CW01477005

Educational Needlecraft

EDUCATIONAL NEEDLECRAFT

UNIV. C
CALIFORN

THE BRIDE.
A PANEL IN SATIN AND SILK BY ANN MACBETH.

EDUCATIONAL
NEEDLECRAFT

MACMILLAN

GREEN, AND CO.
PATERNOSTER ROW, LONDON
BOMBAY, AND CALCUTTA, 1911

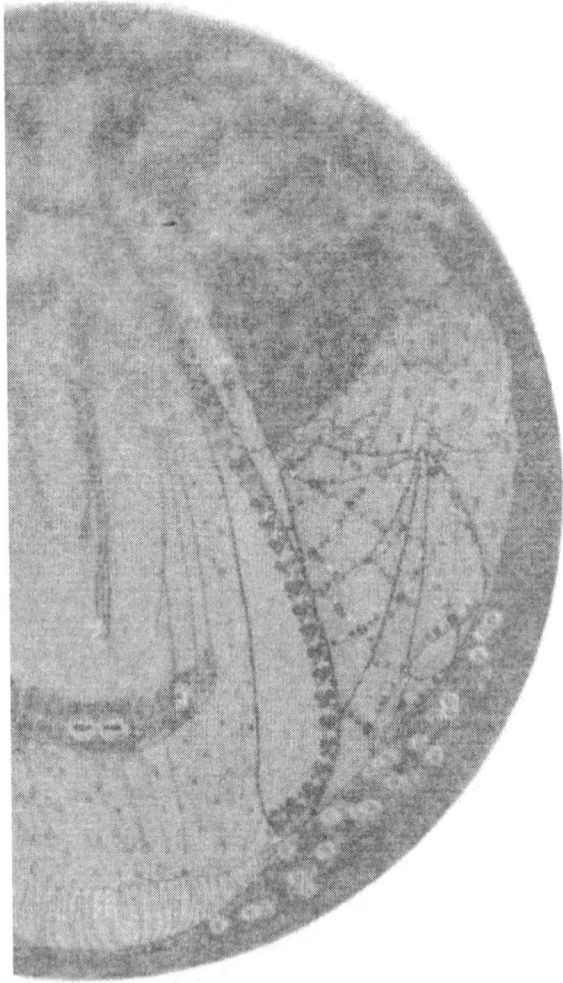

THE BRIDE.

APPLIQUÉ AND SILK BY ANN MACBETH.

EDUCATIONAL NEEDLECRAFT

BY MARGARET SWANSON
AND ANN MACBETH

INSTRUCTRESSES AT THE GLASGOW
SCHOOL OF ART

WITH A PREFACE BY
MARGARET McMILLAN

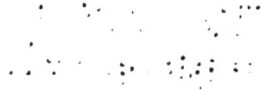

*WITH 6 COLOURED PLATES
AND NUMEROUS OTHER ILLUSTRATIONS*

LONGMANS, GREEN, AND CO.
39 PATERNOSTER ROW, LONDON
NEW YORK, BOMBAY, AND CALCUTTA, 1911

All rights reserved

TT710
58

UNIV. OF
CALIFORNIA

PREFACE

THIS book represents the first conscious and serious effort to take Needlecraft from its humble place as the Cinderella of Manual arts, and to show how it may become a means of general and even of higher education. The writers have faith that in taking the common things of life and walking truly among them they will find greatness and beauty at last. And this faith is justified. Through all the earlier chapters we are travelling step by step and by a narrow path towards a widening highway, along which at last the rapture of life and the vista of beauty greet the wayfarer.

The Key of the whole work is Acceptance. The two authors take the little child as she is—with her long-sighted child eye, her hunger for bright colour, her small, undeveloped hand, her wandering desires (reflections of a brain where even the great connecting pathways are not yet beaten out). They do not ask from her what she cannot give— Imagination without memories, fine or complex work ere yet any real power of fine co-ordination has been won. From the first the child walks with physiologists, who know where she is, physically, and also with artists, in short, with teachers who can understand and interpret her naïve efforts. The knots she makes on her thread with long ends flying might, to some teachers, represent only clumsy method. To Miss Swanson and Miss Macbeth these flying ends are the origin of the fringe and tassel, and they appear on all the early specimens of their children's work. (Later, the fringes of even the commonest things, such as towels, are treated in very charming ways.) They do not even try to influence the little one in her choice of colour, but yield gladly to her selection of bright reds and blues and yellows. The large tacking stitch (which is the oldest of all) done in bright colour on a contrasting background imposes no strain on eye or hand. And thus, without distress, and in the early tracks of the race, the six-year-old needle-woman takes her first lessons.

261094

At every point the joint authors take the main events of growth into account, following the lines of natural development with a new and bold faith, and often *in spite* of tradition.

There is something suggestive of a butterfly hunt in the early chapters, only this chase is not to end in capture but in freedom. From the first the little one plays with what she learns. She plays with her conquests, and takes new flights, and always the helpers meet her at the right moment, fluttering, agitated by the joy of her latest victory, taking her growing energy, and effort, and desire as the token of real success. Surely this offers a contrast to the old method, in which every lesson appeared to add something more to a dead weight that was already crushing the learner.

No obstacle is allowed to threaten the wavering flight of the Imagination—that wide-going, vague flight on which depends all later "Voyaging and Victory." For the educated and full-grown woman, "sewing a long seam" is a good sedative. For the child, sewing must be a flight into the unknown, a joyful adventure, or a fruitless and deadening task. No white seam for her, but bright colours, good contrasts, and when the lesson is over, *memories that do not sleep.* From the first they are awake and stimulate, but it is expected that as time goes on, and many things are learned, these living memories will move in stronger currents, tossed and changed by an inner movement that is never quite stilled even in sleep. This rumour and striving is creative power already. It will grow and gather strength, bringing in its train the reasoning intelligence on which so much depends, and providing material for its exercise. Every part of the scheme is planned and worked out so as to realize this aim.

The passing over from the freedom of childhood and art impulse to real craftsmanship is for the girl as for the boy a new initiation, a discipline. It is due, we may say, at eleven or twelve years old— becomes then a *condition* of any new advance. The physiologist knows that at this age her pupils attain "normal" vision, a more or less adult eye. They are also aware that now there is a sudden development of hand-skill, of the brain centres that represent the hand and its movements. For most children even this great epoch is ill-defined as yet. The blurring of even main lines of growth is the sign of languor in the inner life. To-day the joy of childhood is often hardly present in work. The child mind is becalmed. Strength of impulse is lacking. This is why the 12-year old is not ready to plunge hardily into the cold waters of Difficulty that separate him from the world of real Achievement, but goes on towards adolescence without mastering anything. Our writers, however, do not hesitate, nor do their pupils. These eleven- and twelve-year-old girls do not fail to become real artizans. They seize new tools (the one thing that women have hesitated or failed to do in the past), and with scissors and tape line begin to shape, measure, cut out —in a word, construct. They select types of work, and recognize these in different forms, and in a very practical way go on now to master their craft. Bodices, coats, skirts, collars, underclothing for wearers of every age, hoods also, and caps, braces (the rings even shaped and covered by the workers' busy fingers), dressing-jackets, gowns—nothing is too hard. Childhood's wandering wings of Imagination are now darting wings. All the old learning is in a crucible. Out of mere oddments, and by means of patching and darning, a beautiful new object emerges. There is nowhere a hint of fear, of drawing back, or timid leaning on the teacher. Briefly these twelve-year-old girls are learning *how to clothe themselves and others.*

Social reformers might well glance for a moment at these busy little needle-women. In every great capital there is great display in dress— splendid robes are described in the Press, and the rapid changes of fashion make it needful for thousands of women to appear constantly in expensive new clothes. Side by side with all this, in the poor quarters, thousands of people do not even know what it is to wear a dress specially made for them. Children go to school swathed in half a dozen wretched skirts and bodices or half naked even in winter. They wear old, cast-off clothes, which somehow hide even the grace of child-hood. Yet all this is unnecessary. The elder children—of twelve years— might alter all this in the schools. They could make all their own clothes. Some of them do this already—and more. Without eye-strain, but with free use and application of all they have learned, in drawing, arithmetic, and other "subjects," they have got so far already, that given strong and cheap materials they will clothe themselves and the little ones. To-day our timid pedagogy halts before such an achievement. "Learn by doing," we say, yet even from this diligent "doing" we expect very little. With child-drudgery in all its forms we are familiar, as, for example, with the work of the little "doffer" in the North Country mills. But that a girl entering her 'teens should construct, should take her own measurements, recognize the type of any garment, clothe herself and her sisters, is not expected by many teachers. In vain have the greatest of physico-psychologists declared that the develop-ment of the hand must take place between eleven and thirteen, and that failing this rapid gain in manual skill and executive power in the early 'teens, there is little hope that these will come later. Our guides have been afraid to act on this teaching. The present writers, as we say, are not afraid, but confident. They assume that the brain has its Seasons, and that its snowdrops will not come in August, or its roses fail in June.

Moreover, it is not the child alone who finds acceptance. The writers do not ask for fine materials, but simple things. They decline silks and satins and velvets in the dressing as in the work of children. They take hold of fabrics that can be bought for fourpence-halfpenny a yard, as strong, unbleached calico. They select durable and fast-dyed linens, serge, and flannel. The housewife who knows that she cannot buy expensive things, but only washable and hard-wearing clothes. may well take heart. In the hands of the real artists the common fabrics as well as the common duties take on a new beauty. Not far away must we go to seek the great opportunities, but here in the homeliest tasks—in darning, in patching, in mending. Where there is a strengthening of the work (as below arms, and along edges, or at the end of seams), there is also a kind of blossoming—a fair design smiling out of the practical, well-chosen stitchery. It is all a wonder, this beauty that rises out of necessity and use, and yet it evokes not merely wonder but also recognition. Grave men and tired housewives take up these little garments with the joy that might fill people who go into a splendid house, and then suddenly discover that it is their own kitchen. When one takes those two facts together—the fitness of cheap and common materials for useful and beautiful attire, and the early *power* of children to fashion these garments, what are we to think of the rags and nakedness of our streets ?

In all this new *application* of things seen and done by twelve-year-old workers, throughout all their work now become serious and very practical, the creative power—mother of all achievement—is ever active. Imagination is the leading factor in all work—in planning and adapting clothes as in the phantasies of early childhood. The young crafts-woman works now in many colours. She also begins to touch primitive arts more closely, to experiment not only with materials, but with warp and woof, weaving as she darns, or arranging strands and fringes, so that the darning may be the making of a new thing out of the old. (Needless to say, the darn over nothing or making of warp and woof will be all the more firm and beautiful.) Then she does not march with a regiment, making a dress or other garment that is to be repeated by fifty others. Her imagination plays freely around the work.

She often transforms, say, a pinafore into a dress, or, choosing her own colours in piping, tacking, herring-boning, turns out a garment that has individuality as well as beauty. The joy of labour overflows in the decorating of even buttons and clasps, and above all in the new articles made in holiday mood and in playtime. The sachets, pockets, and drapery shine with a new beauty, a soft radiance that reminds one of the *glow* in the needlework of Indian women. It is the herald of a new life that is fast drawing near. That this approach is indicated, that the jubilant morning song and glowing dawn of youth is found in the later stages of this course in needlework, is in itself a guarantee of its faithfulness.

Where is the pageant of developing human life (once fairly seen) other than thrilling? It is the most dramatic thing in Nature. It should be indicated in the teaching of arts else that teaching has gone, off the lines. Our authors are not only conscious of the rising emotional power that is all around them when the "'teens" are reached, they note its effects in the work. The girl discovers a new way of cutting out subtly and swiftly, a new way of applying stitchery, a new way of treating the folds in texture, ascending from the purely imitative and emulative period to dream her own dreams and see her own visions! Even now the book continues to preach the gospel of the conquest of beauty through common things, and, if its pages blossom (as they do) into a pageant of beauty, the workers are still dealing with cotton fabrics, with plain crash towellings, with simple woollens and coloured mending yarn.

At last the writers themselves, hitherto so unobtrusive, allow themselves to emerge a little. There is a truly *Greek* element in their quick recoil from the use of even the best silks and satins in the house of the average citizen (the highly educated citizen can hardly need or desire costly materials for household things). There is the true Greek spirit in the joyful admission of occasions for splendour and richness of material, but for the most part in communal life, and the whole course of training ends fittingly enough by a study of the treatment of velvet, of "bold and simple patterns in sober colour," for a velvet curtain embroidered with silk in Oriental stitchery!

So the course of work designed to open the girl's eyes to the possibilities of her own home and the beauty that waits her there ends in an indication of the existence of a larger life growing out of the smaller. There is a higher beauty for the mothers and maidens who conceive a great social as well as of an intimate family life, and who wish to give the widest and fullest expression to this higher consciousness.

In becoming good craftswomen girls may become something more. Their work itself leads them to look at last *beyond* their homes, and if they look to-day, what do they see? Much beauty and happiness, work and pleasure, but also beyond these vivid glimpses of widespread misery and darkness—a chaos which waits for creators to make of it a new world. That winged power in them, the unresting creative energy, must find a new field for its labour. It cannot be *confined* to the home. What the educated woman of to-morrow will do we cannot foretell, for she will no longer be the slave of routine and tradition.

MARGARET McMILLAN.

CONTENTS

SECTION I

STITCHERY   CUTTING OUT

SECTION II. (12–14 years)

SECTION III. (14–18 years ; 18–24 years)

COLOURED PLATES

COMMON-SENSE PRINCIPLES
GUIDING NEEDLECRAFT SCHEME

THE underlying idea in all education is development of intelligence and formation of character.

Towards this end, the training of the hand and the eye has to be reckoned with. One method of instruction lies through that ancient and cheap tool—the needle—which gives the **Form** of stitchery; and through material, which gives the **Colour** used in construction and decoration.

Which become one by means of **Art.**

Now, the whole world is plastic, up to a certain point, for the child, and since material in needlecraft is pliable—be it leather or flannel, cotton or silk—the imagination of the child is stirred and curiosity plays freely.

Without curiosity, no conjecture is possible—a point to be noted from the start in all experimental work. The boy or girl who uses material and needle freely in independent design (shoe, cap, chemise, coverlet) ranks on a plane with the scientist who makes a hypothesis, with the artist who makes an experiment.

And the **Form** and **Colour** depend upon the muscular sensibility of the eye. The eye is developed gradually, and we learn to use it but slowly.

The child at 6 years is long-sighted, approaching nearer and nearer to normal vision, till, about 11 years of age, the eye becomes finally accommodated to normal vision.

Only then, and very sparingly, should be used white thread on a white background or any other self tones. It is no more intelligible than drawing with white chalk on a white board, and it throws a strain on eye and temper for every child.

Not till between 11 and 12 years is the awakening power of the skill of the hand felt, when it should be seized at once and properly

B

directed.   During the feeble time, between 6 and 11 years, while the hand and eye are developing and the imagination is strong, the sense of form is big, the sense of colour bright.

All have been artists till now, but specialization in other subjects may come in.   Continuing our subject, however, the craft of the needle becomes not merely a doing, but from this point it may become a personal development both of knowledge and experience.   From 12–14 years inclusive, the acquirement of skill continues, yet it is a period of easy fatigue.

While the acquirement of skill goes on slowly, the girl or boy makes up for that by a greater intelligence, which is much needed at the beginning of the next momentous period, known as " Adolescence."

Thus, any scheme between 6 and 14 years must be guided by —

1. The attainment of normal vision at or about 11 years.

2. The nascent power of the skill of the hand between 11 and 12 years.

3. The necessity for *freedom* in experimental work.

4. The graciousness of **Art,** by which we approach the utilitarian.

" Beauty must come back to the useful arts, and the distinction between the fine and the useful arts be forgotten."

SECTION I

LESSON I

TACKING

AGE 6-7 YEARS

ONE yard of 36-inch wide, unbleached calico, 3*d.* to 6*d.* per yard, will give twelve or nine tray cloths, according as the yard is divided into 12 × 9 inches or 12 × 12 inches. Needles, No. 2 "Scientific" sharps. Thread, No 16 cotton embroidery thread. Cost, 1*d.* each.

Method.—Allow the child to lay and pin the folds down at intervals where the need of so doing is felt ; to construct from the start in its own primitive way. Knots are to be prized in this respect and accepted in all cases, when so expressed by the child in the beginning and finishing of its stitchery. For the first few exercises the child makes under and upper folds equal in size.

From evidence gathered, either playing with oddments in its own home or experimenting with material in school, 99 per cent. begin with a straight line, known as tacking, varying from ⅜ to 1 inch, according as the child is short-sighted or long-sighted.

In accepting and directing this impulse of the child to tack, we avoid that *closeness of range* so detrimental to the eyesight.

As regards colour, the child resembles the savage in his love for strong contrast ; and if he discovers to us his exuberance in crude colour, we may take advantage of this in considering the colour of our material, and direct the child into a right feeling for what is good by *feeding the colour sense* with greens and blues and purples and rosy colourings, avoiding such notoriously hypermetropic colours as red, that intoxicate but do not invigorate.

At this stage and onwards, it should be noted that each child has a thimble and uses the thimble on the second finger of the right hand.

Thimble and needle drills, so called, are entirely profitless. Drills without imagination are a strain on the child and should be avoided.

Diagrams 1 and 2 illustrate Lesson I.

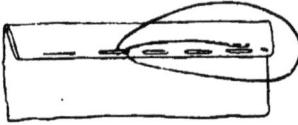

Diag. 1.

Diag. 2.

CUTTING OUT

NECKBAND (IN PAPER)

AGE 6-7 YEARS

"Cutting out" follows naturally from the paper-folding and paper-cutting exercises of the kindergarten occupations.

A piece of ordinary newspaper may be cut out as a *neckband* to fit each child.

The length and breadth of the neck is appreciated, and the introduction of the human model at this stage is justified in two ways :—

1. The child is continually delighted by stringing beads, pips—any scrap of coloured rag which its fancy glorifies, around *its neck.*

2. By swinging the eye to the human form, bit by bit, year by year, a habit of observation is formed during the muscular development of the eye, which gives some idea of proportion and motion. This is invaluable at 11–12 years of age and later, when she deals with the simple **types.**

LESSON II

TOP-SEWING OR OVER-SEAMING

AGE: 7–7½ YEARS

FREQUENTLY during the tackihg together of the tray cloth or small mat the child makes a deviation by over-seaming or top-sewing. This we seize

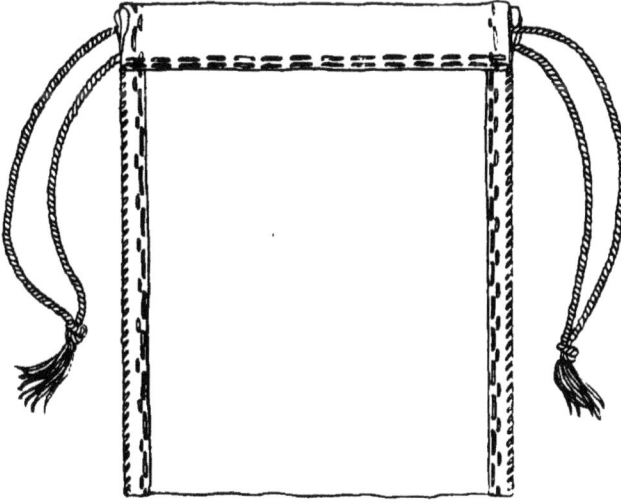

Diag. 3.

upon and apply to the construction of a small bag from the already tacked oblong tray cloth (Diag. 3), or to the construction of a small sachet from a square tacked mat (Diag. 3A). While the child may be disappointed at first to see the destruction of the tray cloths, yet this is changed to joy when she sees the new articles constructed by her own effort from the now well-known tray cloth. Cords may be run through the top folds and used instead of tape or braid, as strings. Children

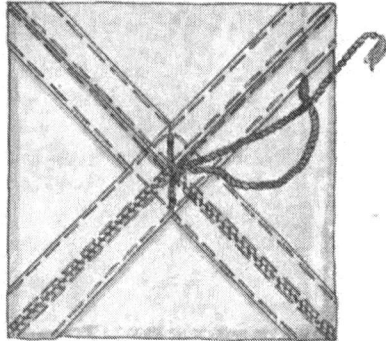

Diag. 3A.

enjoy producing an article which has not existed hitherto ; the constructive faculty is exercised and strengthened.

Method.—The stitch is worked from right to left, and at right angles to the material, which should lie along the first joint and around the finger-tip of the first finger of the left hand, and be kept in place with the thumb and second finger, as shown in Diag. 4.

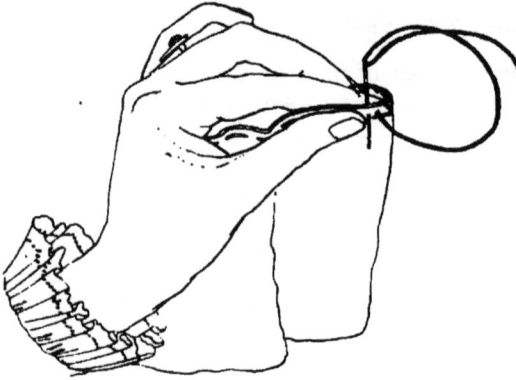

Cord-making.—Two children make a cord. **Or one** end may be attached to a hook on the wall.

They stand apart twisting the strands of thread at each end in alternate directions, either with the fingers

Diag. 4.

or by looping over a pencil or stick and turning round as in 5.

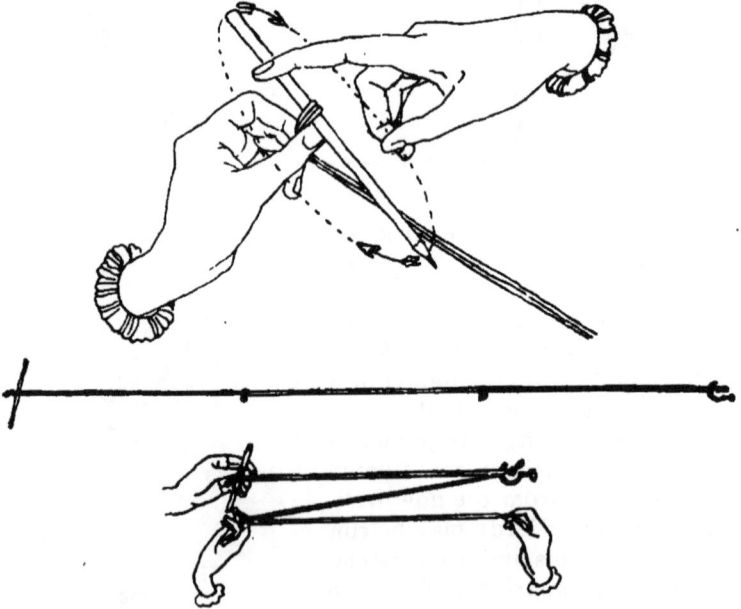

Diag. 5.

When sufficiently twisted one catches the two ends together and shakes out the length two or three times (Diag. 5A).

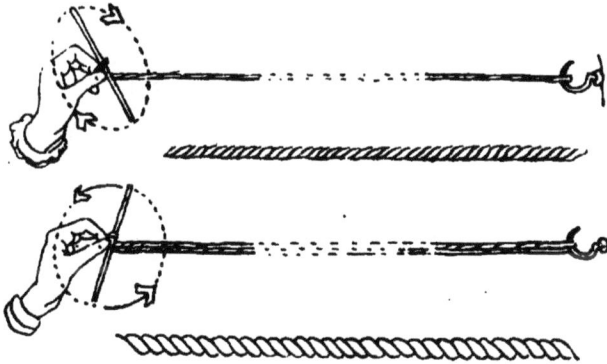

Diag. 5A.

Each end may then be knotted and ravelled out, producing primitive tassels—an advance on the primitive, simple knot, but both serving the same purpose.

CUTTING OUT

NECKBAND (IN PAPER)

LESSON III

HEMMING

AGE: 7½–8 YEARS

ONE yard of 36-inch wide, unbleached calico, 3*d.* to 6*d.* per yard, will give two lap-bags, torn down selvedge-wise, *i.e.* 36 × 18 inches. Needles, No. 3 "Scientific" sharps. Thread, No. 18 cotton embroidery thread. Cost, 3*d.* to 4*d.* each.

The Lap Bag (Diag. 6) is chosen (as a type) not in haphazard fashion; not in commercial aspect; but as a creation from the fusion of the child's knowledge.

The tray cloth, larger in every way, is before her, and the last idea of the small bag paves the way for this expansion which suits the developing eye and gradually less feckless fingers.

Any article with straight edges might be hemmed and the stitch acquired, but needlecraft is much more than an exhibition of stitchery ;

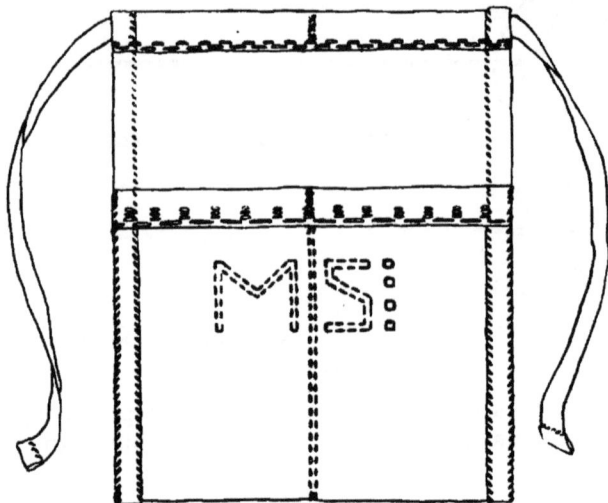

Diag. 6.

educationally the child's mind is being trained through the associative tendency of **Colour** and **Form**.

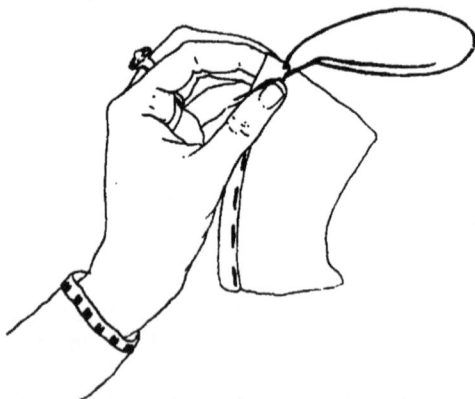

Method.—Lay double folds about ¼ inch in depth, down the long edges ; tack as in Diag. 7 and afterwards **Hem**. The stitchery at this period is an expansion of tacking—slanting tacking with the purpose of protecting raw edges and keeping folded material flat and neat.

The stitch is worked from right to left and shows on the one side as half of a V. At this period, six to eight hemming stitches to the inch, with

Diag. 7.

a rather wide slope, is what the majority of children generally accomplish, gradually getting smaller in size and spacing as the eye nears 11 years of age. Nature guides the child more happily than the teacher to the *right* size; for while the eye of the child is still long-sighted, a certain percentage may have inherited myopia; consequently the stitches demanded by nature in the growth and development of the eye will be larger in the one case than in the other, at the same distance of range.

The edge of the hem should be placed as in Diag. 7 just over the bed of the nail, and kept in position by keeping the middle of the left thumb on the edge of the hem.

The top and bottom folds may be turned to the outside, thereby gaining a pretty, decorative effect, and tacked according to the suggestion of the child's own fancy. The part turned up to form the lap-bag is top-sewed; the initials may be marked with tacking after having been drawn in lead pencil (straight lines as in Diag. 6), though drawing with the needle and thread as the child sews is to be encouraged. A tape is run in for tying purposes, the ends of which may be tacked in pretty repeated rows of contrasting colours.

The beginnings and fastenings of thread may begin now to be tucked in neatly and sewn over; place a ½-inch end of thread along the top between the folds and catch in as the top sewing proceeds. If the thread has to be joined, have both ends lying along the top of the seam and catch in.

CUTTING OUT

NECKBAND, WRISTBAND (IN PAPER)

AGE 7–8 YEARS

The *wristband* in varying depths and widths follows: its proportion to the neck is pointed out—the wrist being approximately half the neck.

In comparing the neck and wrist, distances are judged.

In short, the teacher is beginning to train the vision and the visual memory through short and continuously associated exercises in cutting out; not in microscopic fashion by minute measurements, but broadly by comparing parts of the body quite apart, which suits the long sight of early childhood.

LESSON IV

SEW AND FELL; RUNNING

AGE 8–9 YEARS

ONE yard of 36-inch wide, unbleached calico, 3*d*. to 6*d*. per yard, will give three strips, each 36 inches × 12 inches ; one yard of 30-inch wide dyed calico, 6*d*. per yard, will give three strips, each 36 inches × 10 inches. Needles, No. 3 " Scientific" sharps. Thread, No. 18 coloured cotton embroidery thread. Cost, 4*d*. to 5*d*.

Diag. 8.

This Cushion Slip or Night Dress Bag introduces *combination* of material, construction, and stitchery (Diag. 8).

The period is a very brilliant groping one with the hand, which *tests* as it proceeds, is rejoiced with the combined material, the combined stitchery, and gropes cheerfully, if not surely, with the sew and fell construction.

Assuredly combination is the first element of all creation, for henceforward children *experiment* freely in folding material, and anticipate seams such as counter-hem and run and fell. (This, we continually find in independent work.)

Method.—Allow the child to lay a single fold ¼ inch deep down the

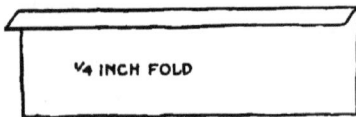

¼ INCH FOLD

Diag. 9.

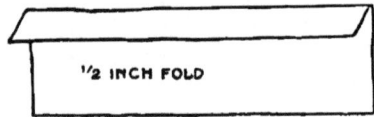

½ INCH FOLD

Diag. 10.

long edge of the coloured calico, and a single fold ½ inch deep down the long edge of the unbleached calico (Diags. 9 and 10).

Place the folds together with the raw edges on the inside and tack.

Commence top-sewing by inserting the needle through one fold, next the worker, leave a thread end the length of a thumb nail along the top and catch it securely in as the sewing proceeds (Diag. 11).

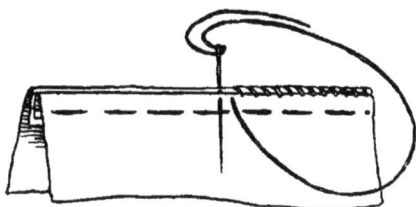

Diag. 11.

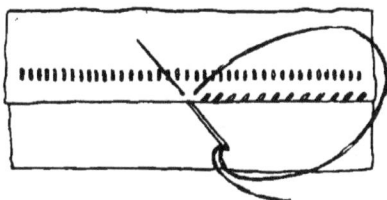

Diag. 12.

Then flatten out with a thumb nail or "bone flattener" and "Fell" (hem), after turning up the ½ inch fold, for about ¼ inch (Diag. 12).

This leads to the construction of run and fell later without breaking the child's continuity of gradual development.

An extra exercise for practice is a suggestion for curtains (Diag. 13).

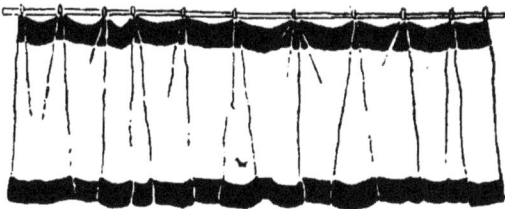

Diag. 13.

Method.—The false hems are run (small tacking) and then turned over to the right side and

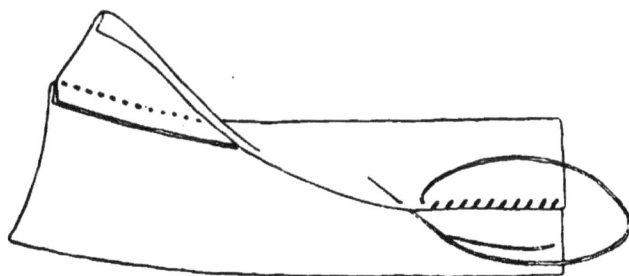

Diag. 14.

hemmed down (Diag. 14) or tacked with one or two rows, according to the child's fancy.

CUTTING OUT

AGE: 8–9 YEARS

NECKBAND: Wristband: Waistband (in paper).

It is astonishing how quickly the children trained methodically to observe and compare can record those observations in cutting out.

The *waistband* follows; depth and width being allowed for, the proportion is taken, which (being approximately double the neck) interests and stimulates the child *to test the proportion* of other parts of the body.

A valuable groundwork is being prepared for the awakening between 11 and 12 years.

LESSON V

PLEATING

AGE: 9–10 YEARS

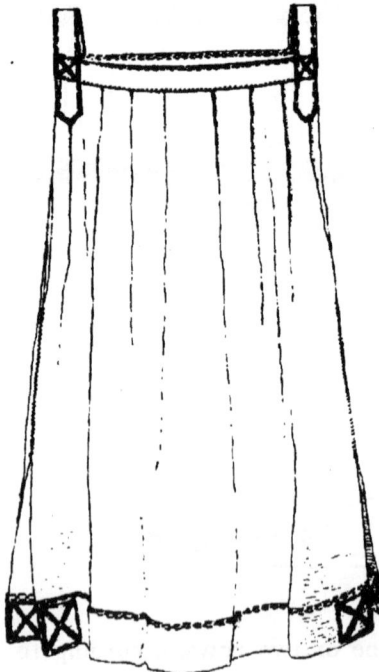

Diag. 15.

ONE and one-half to two yards of 30-inch wide, unbleached calico, 3*d.* to 6*d.* per yard; one-third yard of coloured calico, 30 inches wide, 6*d.* per yard. Needles, No. 5 "Scientific" sharps. No. 25 coloured cotton embroidery thread. Cost 9*d.* to 1*s.* 1*d.*

The overall (Diag. 15) is chosen as a type to illustrate **Pleating** at this stage for two reasons :—

1. The child's free experimental work shows a series of effort and groping which shapes itself in *testing* and *using* the tacking stitch by gathering the material together.

2. The teacher's opportunity to direct this creative quality by the production of the flattened " gather " or **Pleating** in the construction of the overall.

Method.—Finish the bottom hem of each width, either by a false hem of contrasting colour, or a fold of itself turned to the outside and tacked according to the child's own taste.

Note in Diag. 15 how the construction forms the decoration where weight and strength are required, and repeated rows of tacking or top-sewing and hemming effect this in good simple design.

The middle of the front and back width should be marked and the pleats arranged *towards* the arm : three or four on either side to fit the particular girl.

PAPER NOTCHED FOR FOLDING PLEATS

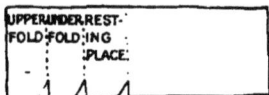

Diag. 16.

Diag. 17.

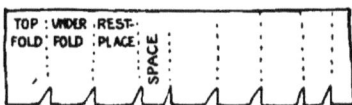

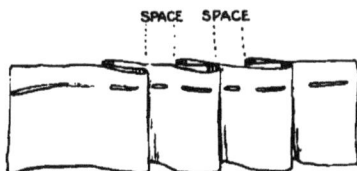

Diag. 18.

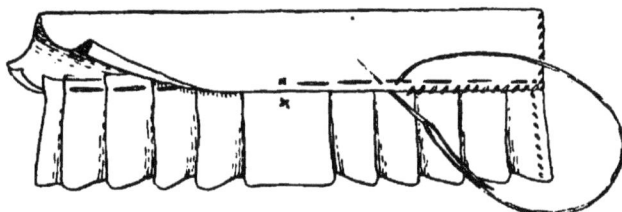

Pleats may be 1 inch, ¾ inch, ½ inch, or ¼ inch in size—the width between being always less with the larger pleat and about equal with the ½-inch size. All pleats and spacings, however, are matters of personal choice : but one pleat should not cover the fold of another pleat, as this would not only be ugly, but impossible to laundry properly.

Diags. 16 and 17 show the notched cardboard or stiff paper which serves as a guide for the folding of the pleats ; the tacked pleating and the

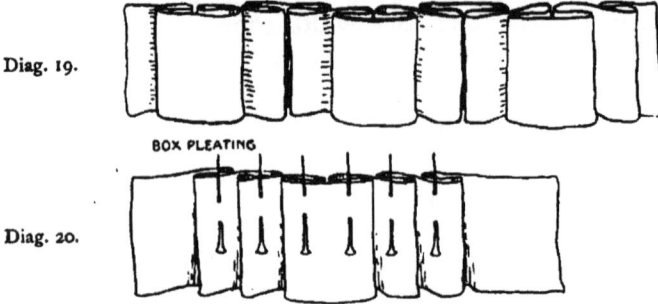

Diag. 19.

BOX PLEATING

Diag. 20.

Diag. 21.

hemming in to the coloured band of the overall (both sides are hemmed) (Diag. 18).

Diags. 19 and 20 show the arrangement for box pleating.

The side seams may be top-sewed for a short distance along each side, leaving room for the arms and legs to move freely.

The shoulder straps of coloured calico may be tacked strongly and beautifully, and connected by a repetition of the bottom hem design.

Diagram 21 illustrates one alternative exercise — Cooking Apron—constructed on the same principle, but with graduated pleating in the bib and strings : the thread in both exercises must be of a contrasting colour. (If the material be extra wide, folds may be tacked down along each side : if rather narrow, the selvedge may be retained and top-sewed.)

LESSON VI

HERRING-BONING

AGE: 9–10 YEARS

ONE yard of 36-inch wide cream flannel, 1s. to 1s. 6d. per yard, will give twelve needle cases 6 inches × 18 inches, and eighteen of 6 inches × 12 inches. Needles, No. 5 "Scientific" sharps. Thread, No. 25 coloured cotton embroidery or fine mending yarn. A small piece of tape, braid or ribbon for fastening the needlecase; a small square of flannel (to be pinked out); and a small square of linen hemmed or tacked for holding needles, pins, etc. Cost 2½d. to 4d.

We now introduce definitely for the first time a second texture—flannel, which has much to commend itself to the child—elasticity, warmth, and weight—and comparing this with the fixed persistent memory of unbleached calico, the child begins to distinguish and *reason*. The joy of a fresh interest in material, coupled with a new kind of stitchery suited to the flannel fabric, is enhanced with the planning of the colour scheme.

Up to ten years of age, normal children do *not worry* about results, and it is important that joyful, interesting occupation should translate gradually this holiday quality of spirit into, at least, an attitude of *alertness*, which is pre-eminently needed as an introduction to the next period, perhaps the most important period in the acquirement of skill, eleven to twelve years of age.

The new material requires a new stitch, and as we began our first bit of calico with tacking, we begin to sew our first bit of flannel with tacking too, but a step in advance of the first primitive movement.

Canvas should on no account be used to practise upon as an introductory lesson for this or any other lesson, till after the eye is finally accommodated at normal vision. Canvas means *counting threads;* it means keeping the material at close range, to the deterioration of vision. Whereas, the eye not only discriminates colour, and enjoys regularity and exactness in spacing through colour distinction, but the muscular sensibility of the eye is strengthened with this feast of varied colour.

"Of all God's gifts to the sight of man, colour is the holiest, the most divine."

Method.—The new stitchery is tacked from left to right in zigzag fashion—a combination known as Herring-boning—one row of stitches on the double fold, the second and lower row on the single material just beneath the fold (Diag. 22). As much material should be taken on the

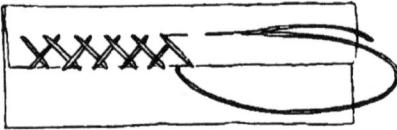

Diag. 22.

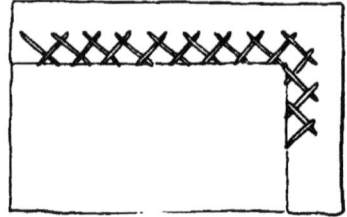

Diag. 23.

needle, as is left between each stitch, and in beginning or finishing threads, "run" the needle on the right side over the last three or four stitches,

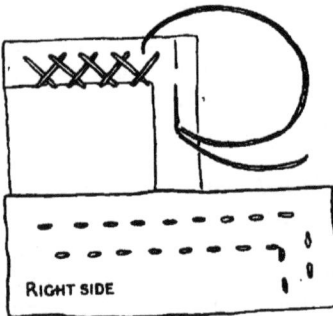

RIGHT SIDE

Diag. 24.

and let the end of the thread lie between the folds.

Note that the pupil be directed to lay opposite sides and to square the corners for strength and beauty (Diags. 23-24).

One end of the needle-case (Diag. 25) is turned up and top-sewed to form a pocket for reel, thimble, etc. ; initials are tacked, and the needle-case is ready as a base for the next lesson.

Herring-boning is distinctly an

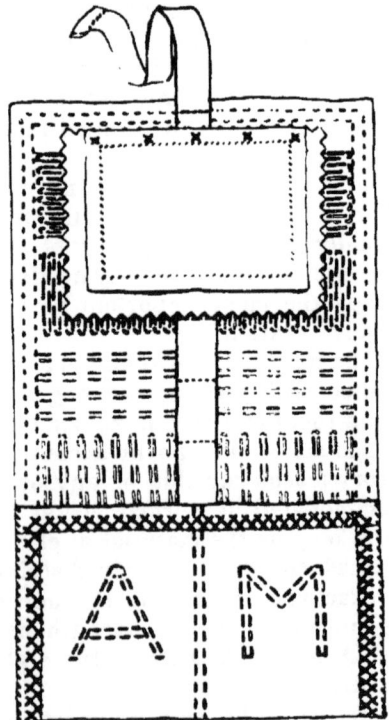

Diag. 25.

acquired movement, and acquired with more or less difficulty; but given freedom with choice of colour and size of fold, the pupil enjoys the effort. Of the value of this stitchery there can be no question.

1. It is sufficiently trustworthy to protect raw edges.

2. It stands in place of an extra fold of cloth, and with thickly woven material, clumsiness is avoided.

3. It is constructive and decorative *at once*, and is therefore an endless source of suggestion to the designer in this and other crafts.

LESSON VII

SEWING ON OF TAPES

AGE: 9–10 YEARS

THE needle-case is our base.

Tapes, braids, ribbons may be sewn on the right or wrong side of the article used, in square, oblong or pointed fashion.

Method.—Right side: *One* of the above forms only should be taught at this stage, and as the square fashion is the easiest, we choose it; the size of the square, of course, is the width of the tape. About one inch from the edge of the case sew by repeated tacking a square at the end of the tape, keeping quite close to the edge (Diag. 26).

Wrong Side: Top sew the square of tape to the edge of the case on the outside, and hem the inner three edges all round (Diag. 26A).

The ends of the tape in both cases should be hemmed or tacked to prevent curling up. A tape may be run the whole length of the needle-case, and tacked at intervals to allow spacing for skeins of thread (Diags. 25, 26B).

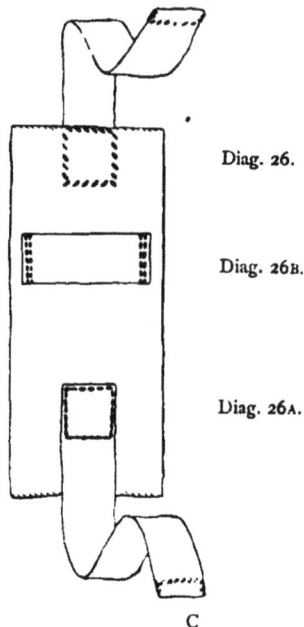

Diag. 26.

Diag. 26B.

Diag. 26A.

C

LESSON VIII

THE needle-case is again the base.

This new exercise stimulates at once by the interesting change of position. The needle moves vertically along the material—up and down.

Method.—1st Position : Up : place the eye end of the needle *upon* the first and second finger of the right hand, and hold in place by the thumb, lifting on the needle the required stitches (Diag. 27).

Diag. 27.

Diag. 27A.

2nd Position : Down : hold needle between thumb and first finger as for top sewing (Diag. 27A).

Darning may be done on either right or wrong sides ; this entirely depends on the weaving of the texture. It is considered better to darn on the wrong side and allow the loops left for shrinking to be hidden ; but as these disappear after the first washing, it is of no consequence. A really good darn should appear equally tidy and workmanlike on either side.

The darning on the needle-case is decorative and useful, at the same time as that part is darned which is most likely to have the nap or ply fall off, and unless darned (fine tacking) at the beginning may probably soon become worn.

Working from left to right is preferred by the pupil. The hand does not cover up the darn, and the regularity in size and spacing is more easily accomplished.

CUTTING OUT

NECK, WRIST, WAIST, ARMHOLE

AGE: 9–10 YEARS

HERE the Arm-hole width is introduced cut in straight fashion. The depth may compare as well as the width with the neckband.

Proportion of neck, wrist, armhole, should be constantly compared and contrasted.

The big step in advance, at this point, is the idea of extra material being allowed for, by *the motion* or action of the arm. This, later on, is disposed of by darts, pleats, gathers, and in Dressmaking and Tailoring by shaping (an acquired and skilful art, quite beyond the compass of children at fourteen years of age).

And it must be kept in mind that while cutting out in relation to the craft of the needle is a separate and self-contained branch of instruction, in another sense, as a natural craft for the child, it forms *a method of instruction* resulting in an intelligent competent man and woman, not necessarily a skilled artisan or a skilled craftswoman.

LESSON IX

FLANNEL SEAMS

AGE: 10–11 YEARS

ONE yard of 36-inch wide cream flannel, 1s. 6d. per yard, will give four infants' first flannel jackets. Needles, No. 5 "Scientific" sharps. Thread, No. 30 cotton embroidery, mending yarn or silk twist. Cost 5½d. to 6½d.

We now approach the period when the eye attains normal vision, and to avoid weariness and strain suggest short seams.

Variety of colour and texture should be introduced, because that increases the interest, be it joy or wonder or curiosity, and prevents the lethargy of the eye induced by monotony.

Method.—The construction and stitchery, hitherto direct—without any complication,—begin now to be a little more complicated.

For this reason the teacher should *demonstrate* clearly the possibilities of the yard, divided into halves and quarters. After some practice in paper, the paper pattern must be pinned firmly on the flannel.

The neck is cut out first, then the sleeve, according to the system of proportion followed from the kindergarten.

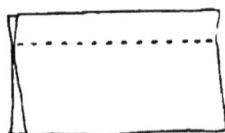

Diag. 28.

The side is sloped straight down the outer edge, and from the top of the portion cut away a triangular piece of the flannel is cut and herring-boned in on each side.

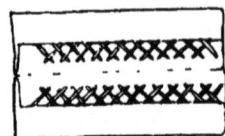

Diag. 28A.

This deepens the shoulders and gives to the worker the opportunity of discovering the advantage of a curve and incidentally the value of a gusset. (The child does not advance with regular steps. We know from experimental work that the work goes on gradually, and the whole advance is made so that those who look on for a little only might declare the efforts of no value.)

Diag. 29.

Method.—The seams are joined by " **Run** and Herring-boning," *i.c.* three running (fine tacking) stitches, then a back stitch (Diag. 28), repeated duly till the end, when two or three tacking stitches finish the running part.

Diag. 29A.

Afterwards, both raw edges are flattened out and herring-boned down as in Diag. 28A, a method of joining flannel always used for babies' clothes because

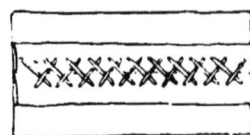

Diag. 30.

of its smooth, flat quality.

Diag. 29 shows a second method of joining flannel, by far and away the strongest method of all.

One raw edge is placed (according to the texture) from $\frac{1}{8}$ inch to $\frac{1}{4}$ inch away from the other edge ; these are first run, and then the deeper edge is folded over (Diag. 29A) and herring-boned.

Diag. 30 shows the least commendable method for seaming flannel, and is suited only for two selvedges or very thick felted flannel.

The squaring of the corners, and the single darning round the neck

Diag. 31.

36 INCH SQUARE DIVIDED FOR 4 JACKETS

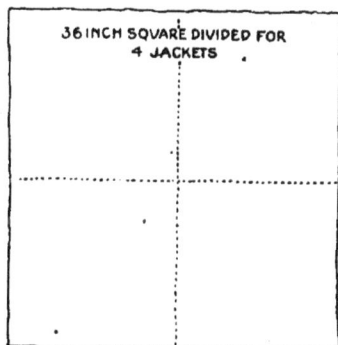

SHOVLDER FOLD

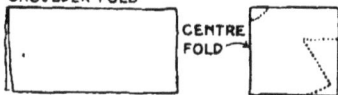

CENTRE FOLD

Diag. 31A.

of the jacket (Diag. 31) where the nap or ply will most likely wear off, show how well the constructive and decorative become one.

Diag. 31A shows the yard of flannel divided and folded for cutting the jacket.

LESSON X.

BUTTON-HOLE STITCH

AGE: 10–11 YEARS

ONE yard of linen 36 inches wide, from 1s. upwards, will give 72 lengths 12 inches × 1½ inches, sufficient for collar or book-marker. Needles, No. 3 "Scientific" sharps. Thread, No. 18 cotton embroidery thread. (This depends on the texture of the linen.) Mats form a good exercise at this point also.

A fresh variety of texture is here introduced—linen—a fabric liable to fray like flannel and requiring a protection for the raw edges, when the linen is of a quality too thick to fold. Hence the knotted stitch, named Button-hole Stitch.

Sewn widely apart, yet strong enough to prevent the ravelling of raw edges, the stitch is known as Blanket Stitch or Loop Stitch (Diag. 32): sewn quite closely together, as in Diags. 33-36, it is known as embroidery or single button-hole stitch.

Double button-hole stitch has a second knot, sewn as in Diag. 37, known as "tailor's twist," and making a very beautiful piece of stitchery.

Diag. 32.

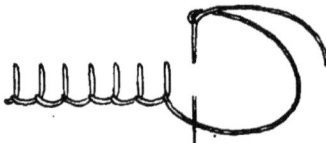

The return to the mind of the sensation of having made a strong, enduring stitch or series of stitches, prepares the mind more and more for reactions.

Diag. 32A.

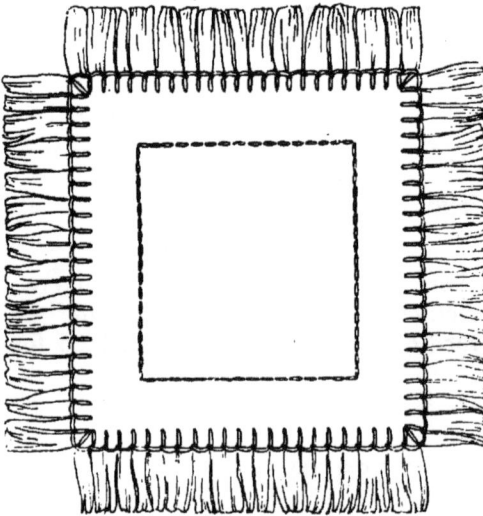

Discrimination between stitchery suitable for various materials is strengthened, and upon the vigour of the girl's mind the creative power depends, moved by the joy of the worker.

Method. — Work from left to right. The small mat suits the purpose admirably. Begin with a back stitch or leave enough loose thread to darn securely on the wrong side. Hold the work over the first and second fingers, with the raw edge towards the worker. Keep firmly in place with the thumb and third finger. Bring the needle out at the raw edge: keep the thread beneath the thumb. Insert the needle with ⅛ inch to ¼ inch space between each stitch, and proceed till the corner of the mat (Diag. 32A) is reached, where the corner stitch will form a diagonal line with the last and first stitch of each side respectively.

In all cases the thread should not be drawn too tightly, as the edges turn up.   Threads should be finished by darning a few stitches at right angles to the raw edge, and fresh threads begun by darning down a few

Diag. 33.

Diag. 34.

Diag. 35.

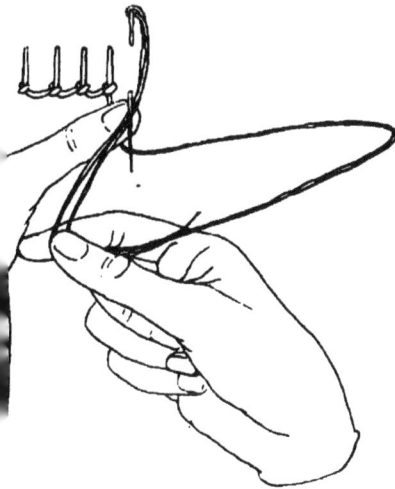

Diag. 36.

Diag. 38.

Diag. 39.

Diag. 37.

stitches in the reverse direction, bringing the needle out at the twist of the last stitch made.

Diags. 38 and 39 illustrate other methods of button-hole stitching.

LESSON XI

CHAIN-STITCHING

AGE: 10–11 YEARS

THE mats, collars, etc., form a base for chain-stitching, which is practically button-hole stitch worked in vertical fashion, for protecting folded instead of raw edges.

The interest of this stitch lies not only in the association of the expanded mechanism of button-hole stitchery and the purpose of strength beneath, but *the pattern-making instinct* of the child responds to the variety, and in experimental work at this period, marking of initials is discovered in varied, imitative design.

The utilitarian necessity is beginning to be appreciated through Art.

Method.—Work vertically. Hold the work over the first finger and keep down with the thumb and second finger; bring the needle through to the right side, hold thread down under the left thumb, insert the needle in exactly the same place as the thread came out; take up sufficient material to form the size of the stitch desired, keeping the needle to the right-hand side of the thread and draw towards the worker to form the first chain stitch.

Repeat by placing the needle into the same hole that the thread came out of, as in Diag. 40.

Diag. 40.

This stitch has many possibilities in the construction and decoration of material.

Diagram 36 illustrates a pattern in chain stitch.

LESSON XII

STITCHING

AGE: 10–11 YEARS

AGAIN, the mat (Diag. 32A) or collar (Diag. 33) may become a base for the practice of stitching—the strongest of all stitches.

This form of stitchery is associated in the child's mind with a former experience in " finishing off," where repeated stitchery meant *security* like the occasional "back stitch" in running and herring-boning; while the appearance recalls the filled in tacking stitch (the original stitch discovered by the child, and possessing always a native interest for her).

Method.—As the best form of construction and decoration means strength and beauty, *a thread should never be drawn in order to keep a straight line.*

Work from right to left.

At this stage the practice is on single material, yet it must be borne in mind that this stitch (containing the idea of strength) is obviously used with double material for joining seams, and finishing the overlapping of openings in garments, strengthening neck and wristbands.

Slip the needle from back to front, leaving a sufficient length of thread to return to and secure neatly (Diags. 41 and 32A).

Place the needle back $\frac{1}{8}$ inch from where the thread came out and bring out $\frac{1}{8}$ inch in front of the thread, making $\frac{1}{4}$ inch in all.

Repeat all stitches in the same way. Avoid drawing the thread too tightly, and at each stitch keep the thread either to the right or left of the needle. Fasten off all threads by top-sewing the last few stitches on the wrong side and bring up the new thread $\frac{1}{8}$ inch in front of the last stitch.

THE WRONG SIDE THUS,

NOT

Diag. 41.

Stitches will vary at this period according to the muscular sensibility of the eye: gradually $\frac{1}{16}$ inch size of stitchery is sewn with comparative ease. All finer stitching should be done by machine.

Back-Stitching wrought likewise leaves a space varying from half the size of the stitch to the exact size of the stitch on the right side, and is much used in dressmaking.

The turn-over collar in Diag. 35 shows a pattern of stitched circles— an approach to one method of sewing on buttons at a later stage.

The colour scheme may be different for each girl, and *her own choice of colour* will give added interest and stimulus, which is not temporary, when she feels herself responsible for the construction of something.

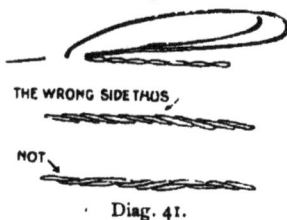

LESSON XIII

BINDING; TAPES

AGE: 10–11 YEARS

ONE yard 36-inch wide flannel at 1s. 6d. will give 18 kettle-holders, 6 inches × 6 inches (double). Tape, braid, galloon, ribbon or strip of raw-edged contrasting material. Needles, No. 5 "Scientific" sharps. Thread, No. 30 coloured cotton embroidery. Cost, 2d. to 3d.

The defence of unprotected edges associates this lesson with *the purpose* of button-hole stitchery and with the technique of an earlier stage, so that the pupil understands values by a natural order of acquisition.

Curiosity and wonder are stimulated, and if those be not fed when most acute, the girl goes without an adequate conception all her days.

Method.—The binding, be it self-edged as in the case of tapes, braids, ribbon, or raw-edged, as in the case of a strip of contrasting material, may be placed equally on both sides, but it is stronger to have the binding sewn on different rows of threads. One-third of the width is hemmed down on the right side (Diag. 42) or stitched (Diag. 42A); on the other side

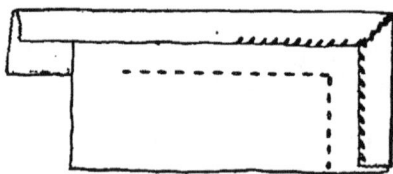

Diag. 42.

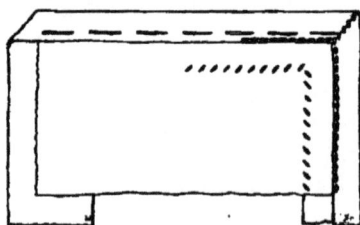

Diag. 42A.

the remaining two-thirds are "run" (tacked finely) (Diag. 42) or hemmed (Diag. 42A). If the selvedge be sewn first, the material has a better chance of keeping free from puckers. Note that the material at the corners is not turned over, all in a fold one way, but balanced so that weight at the corners of the material is equalised and clumsiness avoided.

Half the fold is turned one way and the other half is turned the reverse way, on the right and wrong sides respectively. And in each case the fold is neatly hemmed (Diag. 42B).

Woollen stuffs, besides shrinking more than linen and cotton binding, when washed, are all apt to work in full, which makes it advisable to hold the binding pretty tight; or ease the article being bound, to prevent the binding being full. For very thick woollen and patterned fabrics the binding is often placed all on one side, as follows.

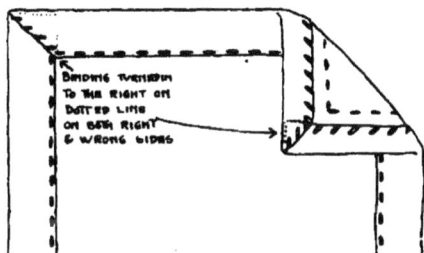

Diag. 42B.

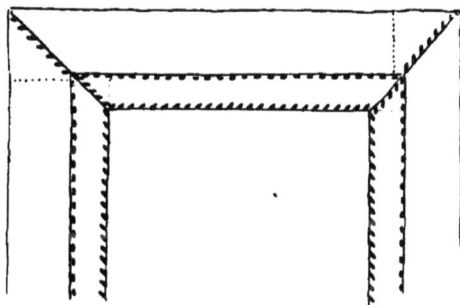

Diag. 43.

The edge of the material is turned down from ¼ inch to ½ inch; the binding is laid over this, keeping about ⅛ inch to ¼ inch from the edge. Run along the outer edge (the running must not be taken through to the right side), and then run or hem down the inner edge (Diag. 43).

Single darning for twilled and irregularly woven surfaces may be practised as an added decoration and thickener to the kettle-holder (Diag. 44).

Tapes. — Connected with Lesson VII, the expansion in making various kinds of loops is much enjoyed.

Method.—The two squares in Diags. 45 A and 45 B should have the two inner edges top-sewed (over-seamed) first (Diag. 45), then seamed to the edges on the right side and hemmed round the three inner sides.

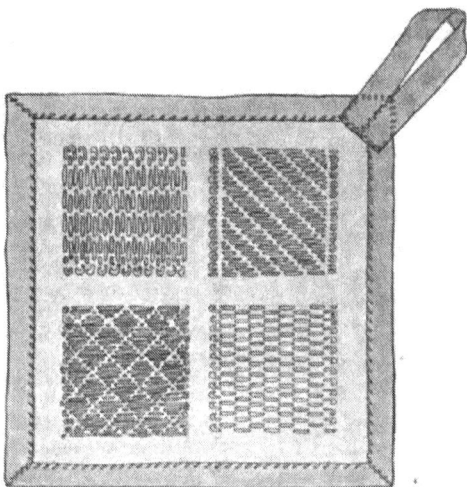

Diag. 44.

Diag. 46 shows tapes sewn as for pillow-cases, when they should be placed ¼ inch to 1 inch from the edge. They are hemmed along the two vertical edges on the inner side and stitched along the two horizontal edges on the outer side.

And as tapes, braids, ribbons, must be placed according to the use of the article, it is well to observe that an oblong shape is needed when the tape or braid is narrow.

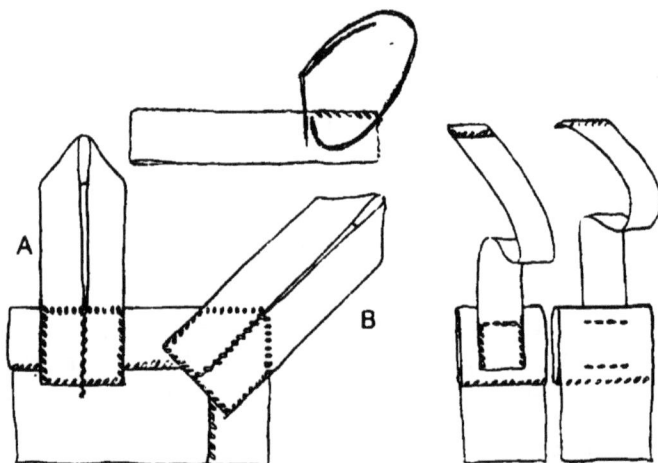

Diag. 45. Diag. 46.

Proportion in binding and in loops is a nicety not to be overlooked. Diag. 44 shows the loop in proportion to the binding.

CUTTING OUT

NECK, WRIST, WAIST, ARMHOLE, BUST (IN PAPER)

AGE 10–11 YEARS

THE child begins to appreciate the value of a smoothly cut edge, as against a jagged, uneven edge—though even with the normal child at this age reversions occur.

The *bust* measurement is next taken—which is nearly the same in size as the waist up to 14 years of age, and in many cases is rather less.

And while experimental work applied to any oddment of fabric, old or new, has been developing on individual lines, the pupils' correction of their own errors—errors inevitable through lack of experience—is bringing them practically to the discovery for themselves of our next step—the *slip-bodice type,* where the ingathering of the various movements is combined.

LESSON XIV

GATHERING, STROKING, AND SETTING-IN

AGE 11–12 YEARS

WE now enter the period of childhood when—

1. The eye is accommodated to what is generally called normal vision.

2. The awakening power of the skill of the hand is felt.

3. The child is prepared to do things intelligently, if it sees the *use* of them, and is willing to devote time and patience to the practice of such things.

But while the majority of children attain normal vision now, a certain number develop slight myopia by over-work at close range—by lacking, in fact, a view for the eye to roam over, and in which to rest.

Thus the girl must be warned against straining the eye, which she is apt to do with her growing knowledge of technique, and that quality of patient industry which makes her willing to devote time

Diag. 47.

and patience to the practice of the needle.

With normal vision we introduce sewing in the same tone of colour and movements that appeal largely to the awakening skill of hand.

A tucker (Diag. 47) is chosen.

The materials may be white or coloured calico or nainsook. Two pieces are required: the band, 13 inches × 1 inch; the frill, 26 inches × 1½ inches. Needles, No. 6 "Scientific" betweens. Thread, No. 40 sewing cotton.

Method:--Take the strip 26 inches × 1½ inches, make a fold ¼-inch deep (double) on the long side, and the two short ends, and hem neatly.

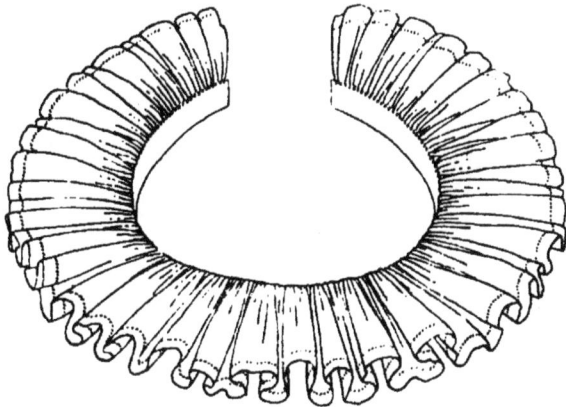

Lay and press firmly down a fold ¼-inch from the remaining raw edge.
Work from right to left and begin on the folded line with a strong back ·

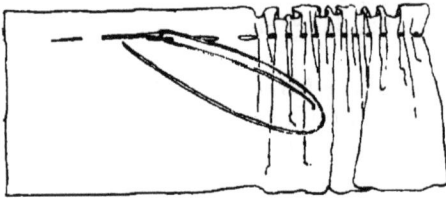
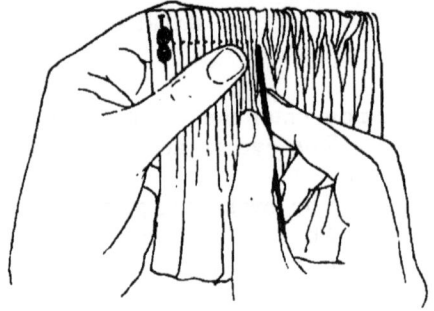

Diag. 48. ·   Diag. 48A.

stitch. Then begin "gathering" by running or tacking, *lifting half of
what is passed over* (the finer the material the smaller the gather, and
vice versâ (Diag. 48).

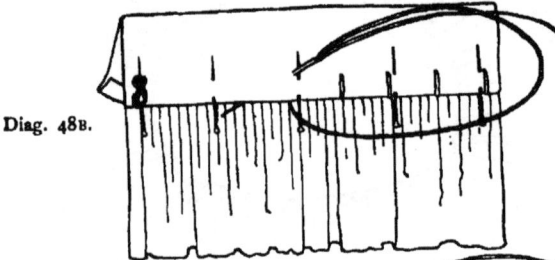

Diag. 48B.

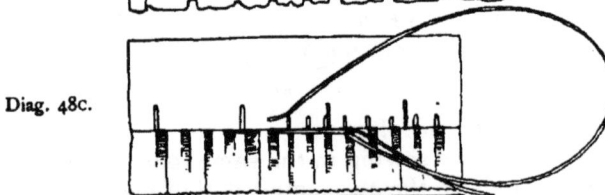

Diag. 48C.

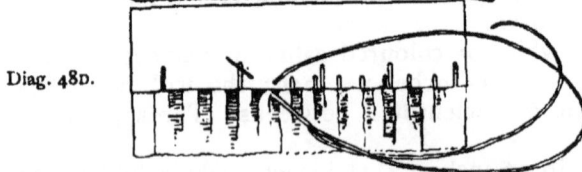

Diag. 48D.

Gather up gently,
straightening . the
material above and
below the line of
gathers, and secure
the long end of thread
around a strong pin
placed at the end
(Diag. 48A).

If the running has
been sewn regularly,
the folds of the
gathers will lie beau-
tifully symmetrical,
as each fold is placed
with the side of a
darning needle in
under the thumb
of the left hand.
This is technically
called "Stroking"
(Diag. 48A).

After finishing the stroking, take the pin out and arrange the gathers to fit the band, tacking in vertical position (Diag. 48B).

"**Setting-in**" has two distinct positions of the needle, *i.e.*—

1. The top of each fold is lifted parallel to the edge of the band (Diag. 48C).

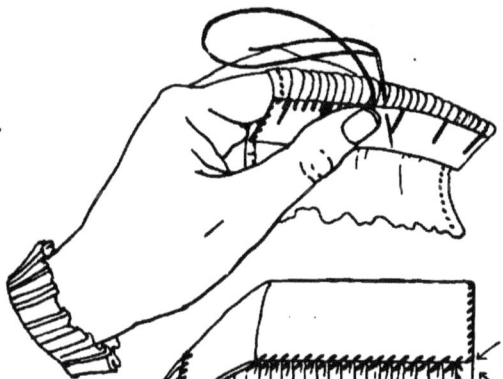

Diag. 48E.

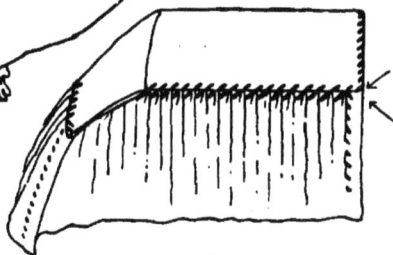

Diag. 48F.

2. The needle is turned up in a slanting position into the band and "**set-in**." Each set-in stitch appears like a vertical hem stitch, lying between each fold (Diag. 48D).

Diag. 48E shows the position of the gathers over the fingers while being "set in."

The wrong side is hemmed down a little above the "setting-in" of the right side (Diag. 48F).

LESSON XV

DARNING

AGE 11–12 YEARS

TOWELLING: rough crash: serge. Thread, Mending yarn of varying thicknesses. Needles, Darners.

Children accept material, be it cloth or bread, in casual fashion.

Their world is full of mysterious things; their uneducated mind assumes that things have always been as they are.

Now, as we have stated, the mind at this period thinks intelligently, though not in adult fashion, and the learner, to understand the mystery

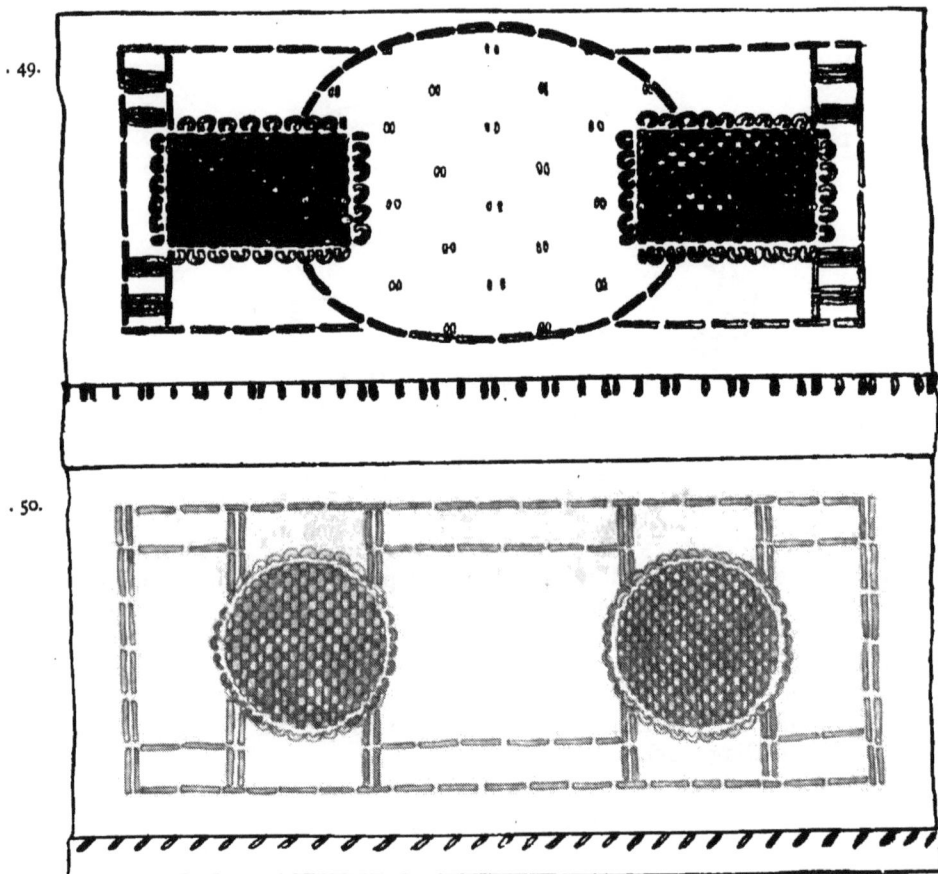

. 49.

. 50.

of cloth, requires the teacher at this point as guide. Here there is an overlapping with history—the first need of man for clothes (wool, cotton, gradually the loom).

And from weaving or darning the decorative motifs in Diags. 49, 50, the child gathers experience, and knowledge, and skill.

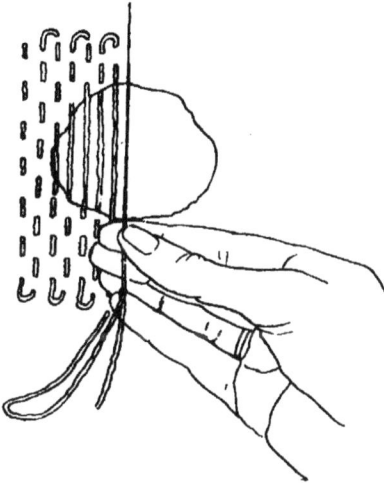

Diag. 51.

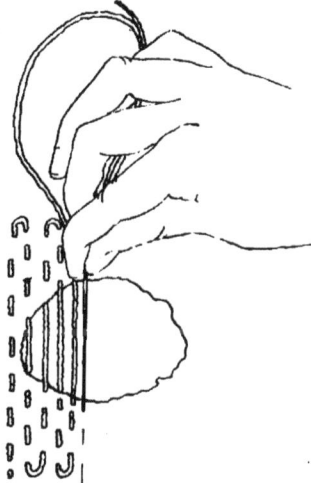

Diag. 51A.

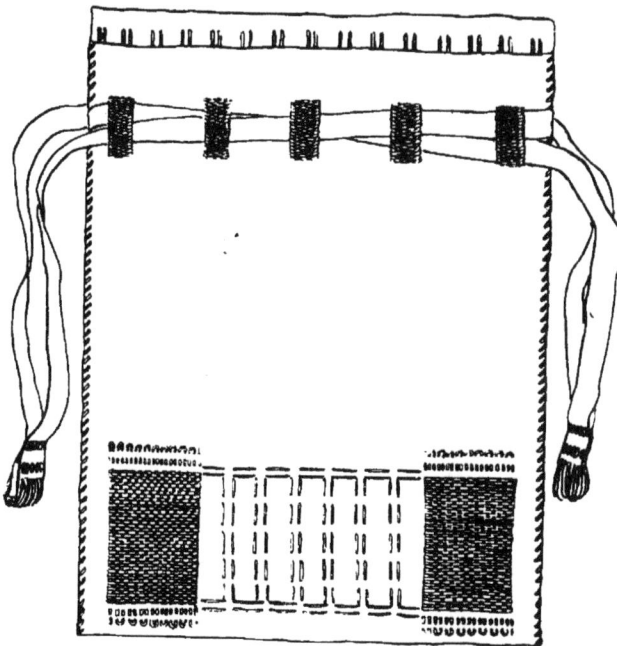

Diag. 52.

D

Method.—Place the work over the first two fingers (which may be separated slightly as the fingers gain control). Hold the material with the thumb and third finger.

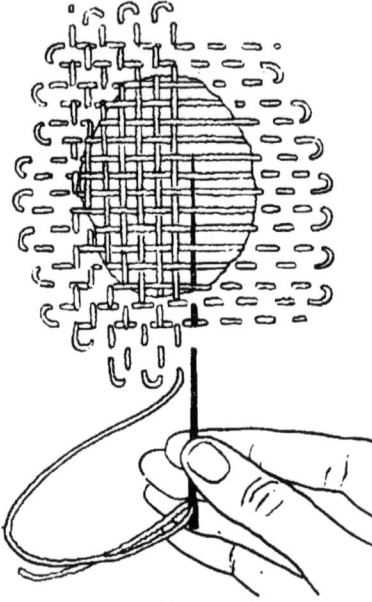

Diag. 53.

Place the needle *within* the hand, upon the first and second fingers, and hold in place with the thumb; darn away from the worker at right angles to the material (Diag. 51).

The needle, as it returns to the worker (always at right angles to the material), is held between the thumb and the first finger as in top sewing (Diag. 51A).

Place in from six to eighteen strands, the size of the motif; then weave across until the tiny web or braid is complete (Diags. 49, 50).

Diag. 52 shows some ordinary darning applied as decoration and latchets to a bag, etc.

Diag. 53 illustrates the second process of riveting the woven (or darned) material on the weakened surround.

And this prepares for the actual hole—darned at the next stage.

LESSON XVI

"A STRENGTHENING STRIP"

AGE: 11–12 YEARS

THIS lesson is the crux of the early period.

The strengthening and defending of raw edges have *followed the need of the child*, and now with the awakening skill of the hand, she seems to have no fear, on the experimental side, in grappling with construction that *needs* skill.

It is the business of the teacher to seize and direct this spurt of dexterity in handling material, or it passes for ever.

There is a second period, truly, when another chance arises for the acquirement of skill, but which, however well directed, remains the poorer if the awakening be neglected.

At this period there is no concern about the ultimate utility of her occupations, and that is perhaps fortunate for the educator.

Flannel, calico, linen, cretonne, any of the ordinary textiles. Needles, No. 6 betweens. Thread, No. 40 cotton, linen or yarn (with darner).

Pockets, bags, child's straight petticoat, slip bodice, can all illustrate the value of "A Strengthening Strip" (Diags. 54, 55, 56).

Methods.—1. Take a strip of tape, say 3 inches. Mark a slanting line midway and cross by this line, forming a V-shaped strip.

Turn in ¼-inch fold at each end of the tape (Diag. 54), and tack down along slit of the garment, which will

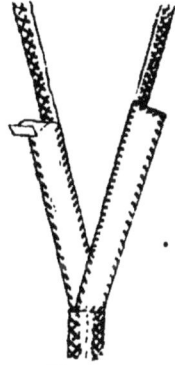

Diag. 54.

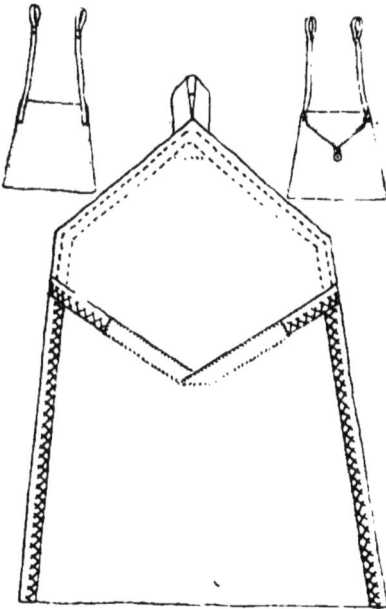

Diag. 55.

Diag. 56.

have corresponding folds tapering to meet the angle of the V-shaped tape.

Top sew the inner edge to the right side of the article and hem down all the outer edges on the wrong side, including the crossover (which should not show the sewing through) (Diag. 56). Note that the tape ends lie in slanting fashion to allow the tape to lie quite straight at the bottom.

To say that only 3 inches of this or that strip is the correct thing is but to reiterate a code of rules, instead of taking the chance as an opportunity for the pupils to show *initiative* and *judgment.*

And that is what we want in all true handiwork : *initiative, responsibility, experiment ;* so, that, like the old Venetian glass workers, our glory will consist in each bit of work being different, showing the power of the individual; not as our glory has been, a machine-like sameness where the hand of an individual wrought—as if the laughter of work were stilled.

Diag. 57.

2. A strengthening strip need not be shaped as in Diags. 54, 55.

It may be doubled and opened out loop fashion, as in Diag. 57, where it actually becomes a kind of tape-bound button hole ; or it may have a piece of shaped material stitched all round, as in a pocket (Diag. 55).

LESSON XVII

SLIP-BODICE TYPE, AND COUNTER-HEM

AGE : 11–12 YEARS

ONE yard of white calico.   Needles, No. 6 betweens.   Thread, No. 40.

The free, bold cutting out during the preceding years, 6–11, has given the girl freedom from rigidity, a necessity in cutting out fearlessly when combined movements occur.

This first type combines the previous knowledge in cutting out, and from the basal equipment in stitchery the girl begins to enjoy the *purpose*, the *variety* and *choice* which the slip-bodice affords.

Towards the human body the girl's observation and effort have been constantly swinging.   Experimental work is exceedingly interesting at this period, and our type follows Nature.   The child has led us from the ornamental neck beads to the blanket with the hole for the head.

Gradually in experimental work, and always with *plenty of room* for the head opening, comes a fitment for the upper part of the body—hence the *Slip-bodice,* which in turn expands into chemise, overall, pinafore, pinafore dresses.

Method.—Tie a tape firmly round the waist. Pin cheap, unbleached calico or scrim on the figure.

The gradual observation from the infant stage shows at a glance that the shoulder is higher than the base of the neck in front.

Allow for this by placing the scrim higher than the base of the neck till the material meets the shoulder easily.

Pin the material on the shoulder and at the base of the neck in front. Cut away the flap of material which falls over. It measures about 4½ inches. This is a valuable little measurement, maintaining the same proportion in other parts of all normal bodies, and should be noted.

The *slope* from the neck curve to the shoulder is 4½ inches. The width beneath the arm from the bust is 4½ inches.

And because of this harmonious arrangement in the anatomy of the figure, we can divide the pattern into three parts.

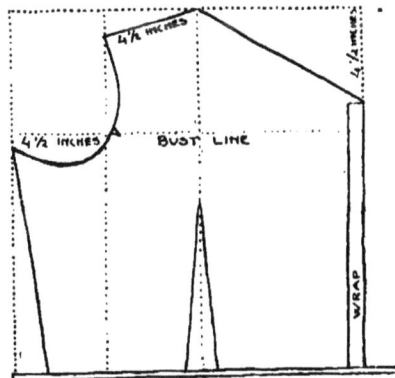
Diag. 58.

As the girl grows older she discovers what is best for her own comfort, and her own ingenuity plans the modifications or expansions of the type.

Thus "fashions" are intelligently followed, later on.

FIRST PROCESS (DIAG. 58).

1. Tie tape round the waist firmly.
2. Turn wrap back.
3. Pin at base of neck and at waist line.
4. Cut off flap at neck..
5. Pin shoulder slope (at neck and arm) and cut.
6. Take in dart 2 inches to 3 inches wide at waist line, tapering off to bust line.
7. Make small notch for the arm curve at the bust line and cut round the arm to meet shoulder line.

8. Cut in beneath the arm to meet the line at back of shoulder.

9. Slope or curve slightly from this point to waist line.

For practice it is advisable to place this moulded pattern on ordinary newspaper and cut out until the girl can cut a nice clean pattern.

Then pin down on the white calico, doubled for right and left sides, as in Diag. 58.

Second Process (Diag. 59)

The cheap, unbleached calico or scrim should be placed against the half back, pinned exactly as the fronts, and cut out.

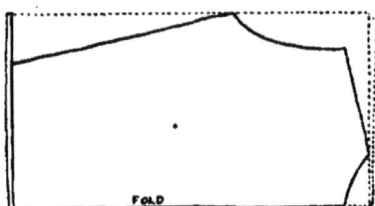

Diag. 59.

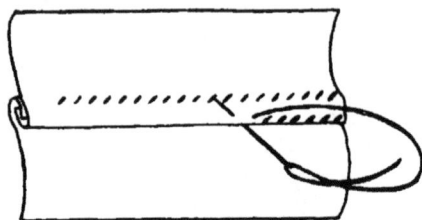

Diag. 60.

In this **type** no basque is allowed, as complications spoil the simple idea of chest moulding and measuring.

If the material should go beyond the waist, merely hem the edges.

The following lessons describe one way of sewing the slip-bodice (Diags. 60, 61, 62).

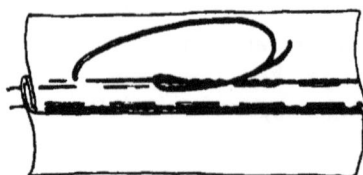

Diag. 61.

Diag. 62.

Counter-Hem

Method.—Join the shoulders of the slip-bodice by a counter-hem, as these being on the cross way of the material are more apt to stretch and get out of place than the ordinary selvedge seams (Diag. 60).

Lay a fold ⅛ inch deep on either back shoulder and on the two front shoulders.

Dovetail both together and allow the girl to stitch or hem the seam.

If hemmed, note that the shoulder hems face each other; if stitched, have the two parallel rows sewn on the right side (Diag. 61); or, another method still is to stitch the seam on the outside and hem on the inside (Diag. 62).

Allow the child to exercise her *judgment* here and choose one method, giving her reason.

Examples of "dove-tailed" wood from the woodwork room might be shown at this point, and in fact, during the next period, 12–14 years, comparisons in all manual work are to be strongly commended.

The child should make acquaintance with the outside world of material generally, even if it can only make bosom friends with one craft in particular.

LESSON XVIII

RUN AND FELL

AGE: 11–13 YEARS

THE slip-bodice makes a suitable base.

Comparison of the different ways of joining, reference to the wear and tear of textures, interest and exercise the reasoning faculty.

The technique depends on the developing skill of the hand, and in this exercise a nicety the child pines for is asked; and coupled with the memory of its own anticipations, this exercise is an unfailing joy and success.

Method.—Turn the wrong sides (the fluffy sides) of the back and fronts *towards* the worker.

Place the two fronts to the back piece—right and left side respectively—with the back edge $\frac{1}{8}$ inch higher than the front edge (Diag. 63).

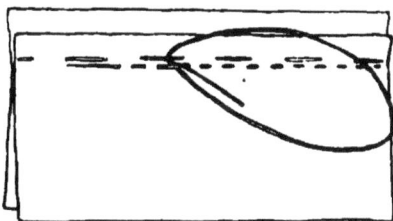

Diag. 63.

Tack both sides, then commence with a strong back stitch and run, *i.e.* lifting exactly the quantity of material passed over, say $\frac{1}{8}$ inch to

$\frac{1}{16}$ inch, along to the end of the seam, when again a strong'back stitch should finish off the thread.

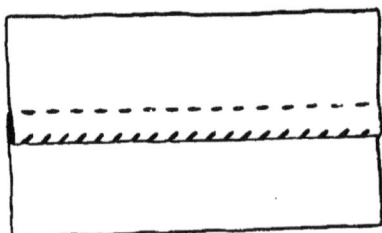

Diag. 64.

Next fold the extra $\frac{1}{8}$ inch of the back over the front edge and turn *flat* down for hemming (Diag. 64).

This seam appeals to the child as only being suitable for lighter weights of calicoes, linens, and washing silks. It is equally suitable in garments and household equipments where there is small strain.

LESSON XIX

TUCKING

AGE: 11–12 YEARS

As far as technique applies, this exercise, like the last, continues the development of skill, and in this respect hitches on to the interest originated with the pleating construction. With this skill the child is gathering *experience* from the purpose of the construction.

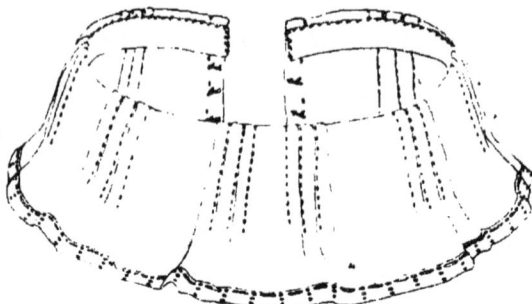

Diag. 65.

Again the slip bodice can form a good base; the material taken in as a dart may be disposed of by tucking as well as gathering in the extra fulness at the back and front of waist. (Experimental work gathered from the child at this period shows pinafores and collars tucked in varying widths and groups (Diag. 65).)

Method.—A small piece of carefully measured off cardboard, notched to suit the size of tuck, may be placed at right angles to the .

material (Diag. 66). Each tuck, varying from $\frac{1}{8}$ inch to $\frac{1}{4}$ inch in depth, should be carefully tacked before being **Run.**

Work from right to left.

Hold the work over the first and second fingers of the left hand, keeping in place with the first and third finger. Begin with one or two back stitches, and then proceed as in running. One to three stitches may be lifted at one time, as the hand gains in dexterity.

At the last running stitch, take a back stitch and run in the thread over the last two or three threads and snip off neatly.

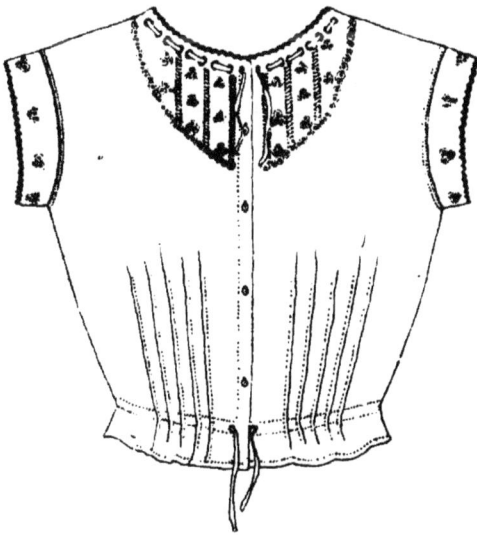

Diag. 66.

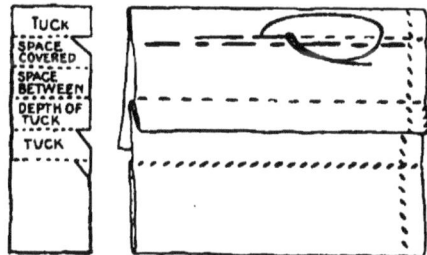

Diag. 67.

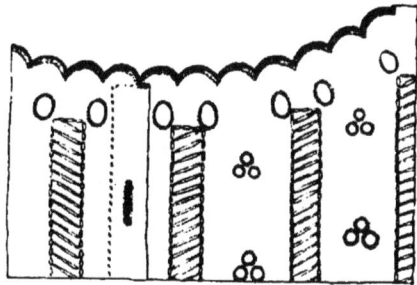

Diag. 67A.

Begin a new thread by slipping the needle between the folds, and bringing it out two or three stitches *to the right* of the last stitch ; take a back stitch, run over the last stitches made on the underfold, and proceed as before.

It is important in all running of tucks that the thread goes right through the folds, giving a similar appearance on the upper and under fold.

Tucks may also be hemmed or machine stitched.

They may be treated singly, as in Diag. 67, or in groups, as in

Diag. 65; but with any arrangement it should be carefully noted that tucks must not be allowed to overlap one another.

Tucks vary in width from ⅛ inch in fine cambric to 2 inches in woollens and prints.

LESSON XX

SEWING ON OF BUTTONS

AGE: 11–12 YEARS

THE slip-bodice again is the base upon which to sew the button and sew in the button-holes.

As a preliminary, a strip of tape may be taken, long enough to be used as a book strap—one end doubled up, and a few buttons sewn on sufficiently spaced to allow for few or many books.

Buttons are of endless variety—with and without stems or shanks.

Method.—Without stems and unpierced they are sewn—

1. By a simple cross (Diag. 68 F).
2. By a star (Diag. 68 B).

And for both, after making a small back stitch, bring the needle up *through the centre* of the button with each stitch made.

These and the following require to be sewn loosely, to allow three or four threads to *stem* or tie the stitchery together as a cord. Besides adding strength to the button, the stem gives room for the button-hole *to lie flat* beneath (Diag. 68 I).

Other methods are shown in Diag. 68 (A, C, D, E, G), parallel bars stitched, and buttoned-holed; small circle stitched.

For chintzes, cretonnes, and similar weight of material, the stitched circle is not to be recommended, as it puckers up and tends to tear away the heavy material during the cleaning processes.

Button moulds are covered with a piece of material about ¼ inch larger than the mould all round. This is run about ⅛ inch from the edge, gathered up and secured by one or two back stitches.

As a stem for the button, sew two button-holed bars crossing in the middle at right angles.

Top sew this at the centre and for a little on each side to the garment (Diag. 68 H).

Pierced linen buttons are sewn—

STEMMING

Diag. 68.

1. By three stitches crossed.
2. By parallel bars stitched.

LESSON XXI

SEWING OF BUTTON-HOLES

AGE: 11–12 YEARS

THE book strap of last lesson, or book mark (Diag. 69), may serve as preliminaries to the slip-bodice, which again serves for this application.

The developing skill of hand *enjoys* the nicety demanded in the finish of a button-hole, and the *technique acquired now is never lost*, which is important, when we realize that our part is to supply such for the later stage of life and development.

Method.—Make a slit by doubling up the cloth and cutting with a small sharp pair of scissors ¼ inch to ⅜ inch in a perfectly straight line.

Open out. The button-hole should be worked (like the mat and collar) with the raw edge *towards* the worker, and if desired double button holed (tailor's twist).

The button-holes may be finished first with round ends—having three stitches over-seamed in a slanting direction on either side of the three stitches that lie almost in a straight line at each end (Diag. 70B).

Braced ends are supposed to be stronger. They are button-hole stitched at right angles to either end of the button-hole (Diag. 70A).

These varieties are placed vertically in the fronts of pleats, wraps, etc.

The button-hole with the braced and round end (Diag. 70C) is generally placed at one end of a band, for two reasons: 1st, The round end allows the button to lie smoothly. 2nd, The braced end is supposed to be stronger in resistance than the round end.

Note, if the thread should break while sewing a button-hole, undo one or two stitches and work the end in by darning above the edge of the button hole.

Slip the fresh thread in by darning in the reverse

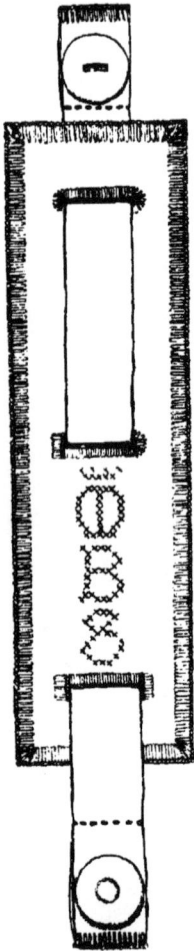

Diag. 69.

direction and bringing the needle out in the middle of the last button-hole stitch made..

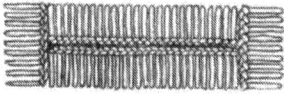 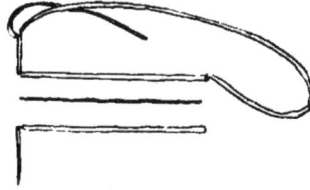

Diag. 70A.

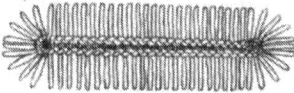 

Diag. 70B.

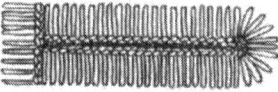

Diag. 70C.

Diag. 70.

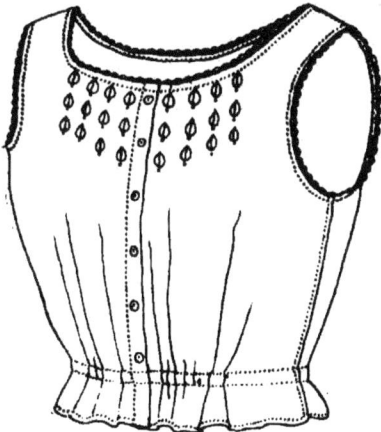

Diag. 71.

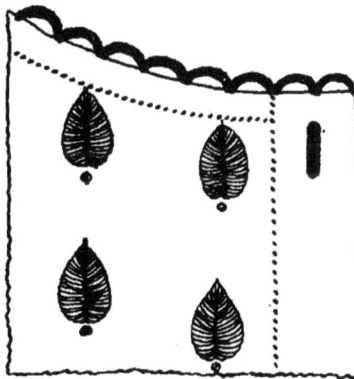 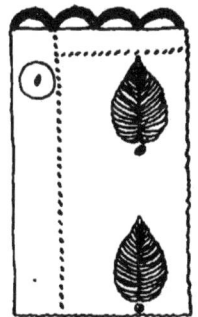

Diag. 71A.

The slip-bodice that has served as a base for these applications may be finished in a different way by each girl.

The sewing of the neck and armholes may be so constructed as to form the decoration; the plain surface above the bust allows for the pattern-making instinct, and is a chance for displaying much ingenuity (Diags. 71, 67A).

(All kinds of slim machine-made lace should be avoided; it becomes frayed and torn with washing, and proves most unsatisfactory.)

During the whole period from 11 to 12 years of age the cutting out of the slip-bodice type should be constantly practised, and memorized.

SECTION II

LESSON I

AGE: 12-14 YEARS

THIS is the slack period before the spurt of adolescence.

Greater stability, deliberate movement, above all *the brooding quality* characterizes the girl, and must not be interfered with, unless to the *arrest* of developing organism.

Therefore, finicking, petty, troubling work should be avoided. A broad, general view of things should be adopted. In the realm of handiwork, minute measurements should give place to general proportions and interesting comparisons.

To the slip-bodice type, we hang on the sleeve type, giving in this manner the nucleus of blouse, jacket, or nightdress.

A general talk on sleeves, short, elbow, three-quarter, full length, as they are used for chemise or nightdress, blouse or coat, should precede the Type, from which all these may be expanded or modified.

Method.—1st Movement. The girl places one end of the tape line on the shoulder, bends the arm (to allow for the expansion of the arm at the elbow), and brings the tape a little way beyond the wrist (Diag. 72). Say this measurement is 24 inches; draw *the length* on the blackboard.

2nd Movement. Take *the width* by encircling the shoulder with the tape (Diag. 72B), allowing from 2 inches to 3 inches for thickness of clothing.

This measures probably 28 inches. Draw the width on the blackboard. One sleeve thus measures 24 inches × 28 inches.

Double this up in ordinary newspaper or draw on blackboard to represent the upper and under sleeve.

In *proportion* to the length, the elbow occurs about the middle — this *halves* the sleeve, and when the arm is swung freely about one-quarter of the length is allowed for *the motion* at the shoulder. As the child has

47

been led gradually from the earliest to consider one part of the body in relation to another part—*the relative proportion* of the wrist to the armhole

Diag. 72A.

Diag. 72B.

Diag. 72.

is remembered as being half the width, and again one-quarter extra is allowed for *the motion* of the wrist and the width of the shut hand (if made without side openings).

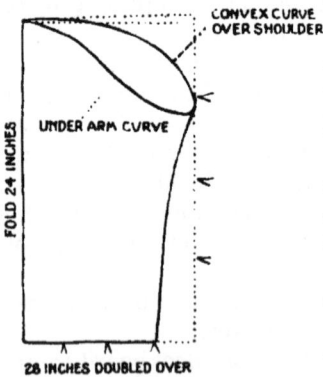

CONVEX CURVE OVER SHOULDER

UNDER ARM CURVE

FOLD 24 INCHES

28 INCHES DOUBLED OVER

Diag. 73.

Draw a slightly curved line on the three-quarter length to meet the three-quarter width at the wrist (Diag. 73). Cut by this line in paper.

Draw attention to the contour of the shoulder, and draw the convex curve to indicate the shoulder top (Diag. 73). By this line cut both upper and under sleeve.

Next draw and cut away the under arm (Diag. 73).

The type is now ready for application. Modifications and expansions occur later.

(Ordinary newspaper does very well for practice, before cutting out in the selected material.)

Note, in cutting out a pair of sleeves according to the **Type**, to have the right sides facing each other—wide enough material to be folded by the warp ; narrow material to be folded by the weft.

LESSON II

FRENCH OR BODICE SEAM (BOY'S COAT)

AGE: 12–14 YEARS

THE sleeve type hung on to an expansion of the slip-bodice type combines as a coat suitable for a child of six years (Diag. 74).

The stitchery and construction used for this seam appeals by its quality of expectancy, very specially in the 13th year, and precedes *as an* .

Diag. 74.

exercise in machining for the more advanced motor control required in the finishing of bottom hems, wristbands, neckbands, etc., later on.

Method.—Place the raw edges together, wrong side facing wrong side.

Tack fully ⅛ inch beneath these edges : then run with the hand or machine-stitch.

E

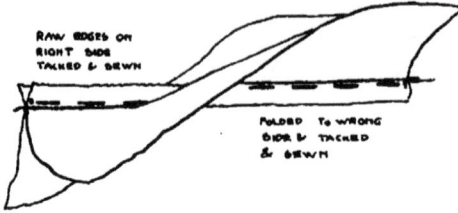

RAW EDGES ON
RIGHT SIDE
TACKED & SEWN

FOLDED TO WRONG
SIDE & TACKED
& SEWN

Diag. 75.

Remove tacking thread and turn the raw edges to the inside.

Tack again about $\frac{1}{4}$ inch from the double-folded edge, and back-stitch or machine-stitch, along by the tacking thread (Diag. 75).

This seam should always be used in joining material that frays easily. In all skirts, pinafores, and blouses it is a very valuable seam.

LESSON III

GUSSETS (DRESSING JACKET)

AGE: 12–14 YEARS

THE principles underlying the overall, the infant's first flannel jacket, and now the child's coat, tend to give that ability which results in a wider application.

In Diag. 76, with the wider application of Dressing Jacket, we

Diag. 76.

have the gusset introduced as well as crossway bands sewn in varied ways.

(Incidentally, if a mistake should happen, as it may, the girl has shown in experimental work how from the mistake may issue something new and equally good.)

Gussets are double shaped, single square, and single triangular.

The double-shaped gusset is the most enduring of all, and is used very exclusively for boys' and men's shirts.

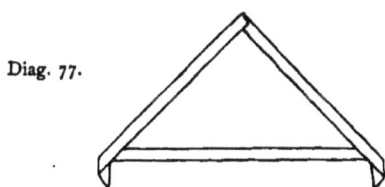

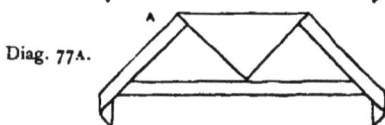

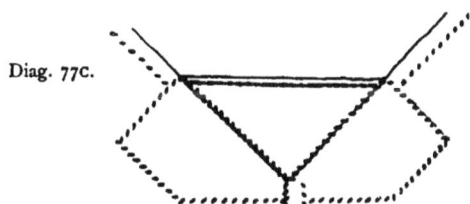

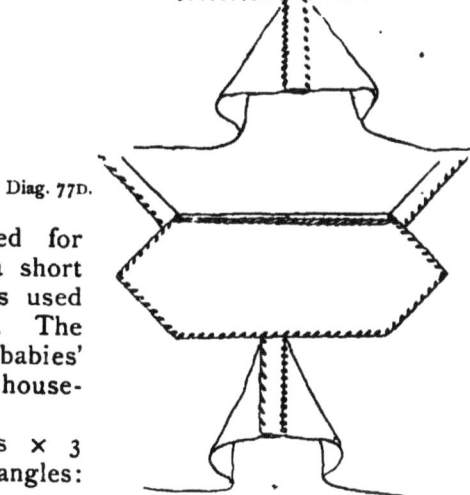

Diag. 77.

Diag. 77A.

Diag. 77B.

Diag. 77C.

Diag. 77D.

The single square is used for widening the under part of a short chemise sleeve ; and doubled is used for the necks of boys' shirts. The single triangular is used for babies' clothes, and articles of general household needs, as bags.

Method.—Material 3 inches × 3 inches is taken, halved in two triangles: ready to make a pair of gussets.

Turn down a fold $\frac{1}{8}$ inch round the triangle on the wrong side (Diag. 77A). Turn down the apex to the middle of the base and crease the fold (Diag. 77A).

Turn up the ends of the base to meet the fold, and cut off this turned-up part $\frac{1}{4}$ inch from the outer fold (Diag. 77B).

Place the apex of the gusset at the end of the *seaming ;* over-seam the two sides of the gusset to the garment, as far as the middle fold (Diag.

77C); turn over the lower half of the triangle to the inside, hem neatly all round and stitch across the edge of the middle fold, which should be stretched slightly to make it lie flat (Diag. 77D).

The square gusset used for widening and strengthening the under arm of garments is set in by a stitched counter-fold.

Diag. 76 illustrates both methods.

LESSON IV

CROSSWAY STRIPS.   FRENCH KNOTS

AGE: 12–14 YEARS

HITHERTO strips cut selvedge-wise for strength and easy manipulation have been practised, but as the constructive and inventive power expands the straight line is superseded by curves for a time, and experimental

Diag. 78.

work is extremely interesting between 12 and 14 as a fruitful period in curves.

One difficulty in technique to the *brooding, easily fatigued* girl, is how to strengthen this curve in the plastic material, which she cuts out, and is overcome by the introduction of a cross strip.

·The bias or cross-cut quality of stretchiness and strength impresses them at the right moment, and consequently a vigour is gained which cannot be lost.

The curves of armholes, neckbands, foot of skirts, coats, etc., may all be finished in a strong, beautiful manner, enhanced with stitchery,

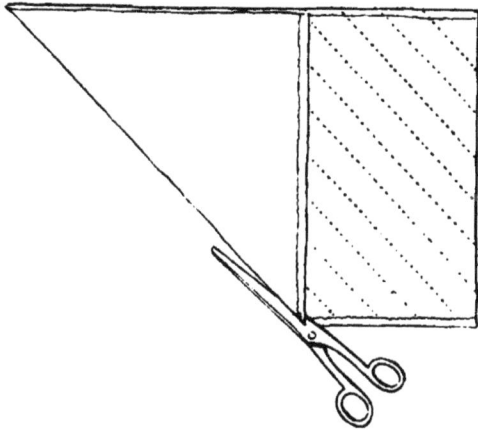

Diag. 79.

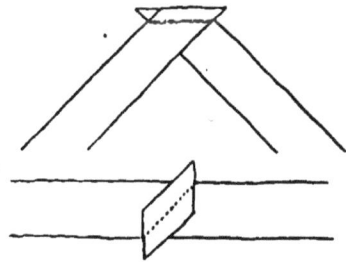

Diag. 80.

tacked or hemmed in groups (Diag. 78).

Method.—Diag. 79 shows how strips may be cut cross fashion.

Placing the sharp angle of the strip to the blunt angle, the strips are joined by a strong back stitch; then flattened out and stretched to fit the curve (Diag. 80).

The cross strip is placed next the worker, tacked and machined, then turned over, either to the right or wrong side, according to the purpose of the garment, and finished according

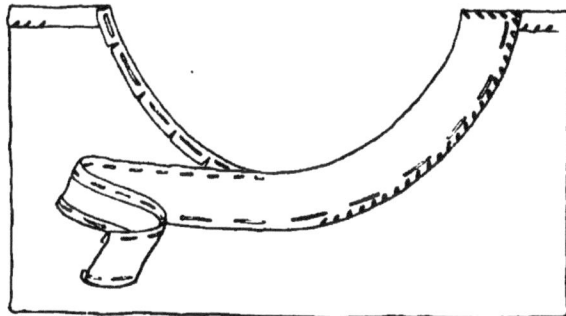

Diag. 81.

to the taste of the worker by one or more of the many stitches now at her disposal (Diag. 81).

French Knots.—Back-stitching and button-hole stitching *expand* into a *very strong* and *very beautiful* row or rows of stitchery.

Method.—Hold work as for hemming. Work from right to left (beginning with a strong back stitch). From the place where the thread comes out, allow the thread to lie in a perfectly straight line to the left for about ¼ inch and keep firmly down with the thumb. Slip the needle underneath this thread from above (Diag. 82).

Turn the needle in circular fashion from right to left, until it goes quite round to the place where the thread came out (Diag. 82A). Insert

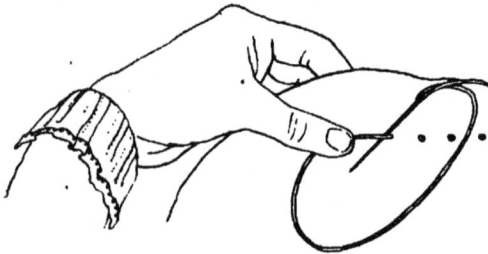 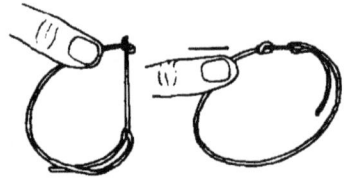

Diag. 82.   Diag. 82A.   Diag. 82B.

through the material at this point and come out as in stitching; spaced according as the purpose of the article demands—from the area of the knot, say to an area of ¼ inch (Diag. 82B).

For a thick knot it is better to work with two single threads and a rather larger-eyed needle, than with a thread doubled, because the latter is apt to knot and twist and generally trouble the worker.

Finish off as in stitching.

It is a mistaken custom to twist the thread several times round the knot in order to make a larger size, as the twisting tends to make loose and untidy knots and is a far less speedy and regular method.

LESSON V

PIPING

AGE: 12–14 YEARS

PIPING is closely associated with the foregoing lesson.

1. The material is cut so that the stretching quality of the bias or cross may allow the cord to lie without puckering the piping.

2. Curved edges and seams are finished in a strong, beautiful way.

Method.—Ordinary string, staycord, *any round*, thickish compact thread may be used, as this rib which is encased in the cross-way material, protects and beautifies.

'Place a ½-inch cord, ¼ inch from the top edge of the wrong side of the cross strip of material; fold this edge over the cord and tack closely under the roll (Diag. 83).

Diag. 83.

Place the piping downwards on to the right side of garment, about ¼ inch from the edge.

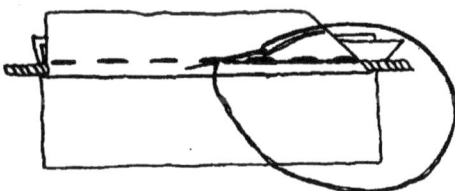
Diag. 83A.

Note that the top corner of the cross strip is at least ¼ inch from the edge of the garment.

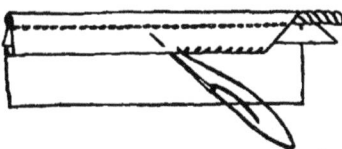
Diag. 83B.

Back stitch close up to the cording (Diag. 83A).

Flatten out the cord to the right side.

Where the garment is not to be lined, the outer raw edge should be folded in and hemmed down (Diag. 83B).

LESSON VI

SKIRT TYPE

AGE: 12–14 YEARS

JUST as the Sleeve Type never alters in principle, however numerous the varieties, so with the next type.

The **Skirt** may be a modified form known as an under petticoat, made up in woollen material; it may be expanded and called a top petticoat, made up from one of the many varieties of cotton or silk manufactures.

It may be cut in one or in many pieces, but the girl who has been taught to make the simple **Type**, with

Knowledge of (1) Proportion and (2) Motion ; that sense of beautiful
   form (lines, curves, mass, etc.) which depends on *the muscular
   sensibility of the eye,*
is able not only to imitate and emulate the **Type**, but dreams and devises
with interesting expansions.

The *interest* roused by the many varieties of manufactured material,
flannel, nun's veiling, lustre, calico, nainsook, print, silk, moirette, etc.,
should be made the most of in relation to the elementary types.

For example—

 1. The *age* of the wearer.

 2. *Season of the year* in which the garment is to be worn.

 3. *The width* of woollens, cottons, silks and mixtures, such as
Union.

 4. *Right and wrong sides* (as the nap or pattern may very decidedly
show) lead us to consider reversible or non-reversible stuffs in relation
to *economy.*

This, of course, is a borrowed interest ; it becomes interesting through
its association with the *constructions* in which an interest already exists.

And when we realize that the *idea* springs from the doing ; that there
is no limit to the associative expansions of the idea either under the wing
of joy or with the scent of danger not far away, we see how careful of
the **Type** we must be, for in endless ways the expansion may result.

Method.—$1\frac{3}{4}$ yards to $2\frac{1}{2}$ yards, 36 inches wide, give a skirt of light
weight. *According to one's height* skirts vary from $1\frac{3}{4}$ yards to 3 yards.
(If the foot be finished with flounce or frill 1 to 2 yards more will
be required.)

According to age, the *length* is taken from waist to *calf, ankle,* or *toes.*

(Skirts to the knee are cut straight, gathered or pleated into a straight
band to fit round the waist (Diag. 56).)

The width depends on the motion of the body : in relation to its
proportion, the longer the skirt the wider it will be round the foot.

The difference between what a skirt demands when the person is
sitting and when the person is walking must be considered, since room
to step out demands a certain width, and this, of course, is in proportion
to length of limb ; so that the girl not only *measures*, but must be on the
alert for the why and wherefore—the double intellectual effort.

Cut off two widths the required length.

Double both widths selvedge wise.

Allow twice as much to the width at the foot (*room for stepping out*) as
what is allowed at the waist (Diag. 84).

Note the gradual slope from the back to the front.

Place the selvedge to the slanting edge and cut away the extra flap at the foot, following the circular shape of the garment.

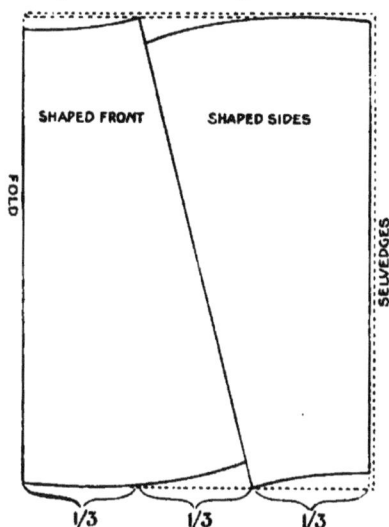

Diag. 84.

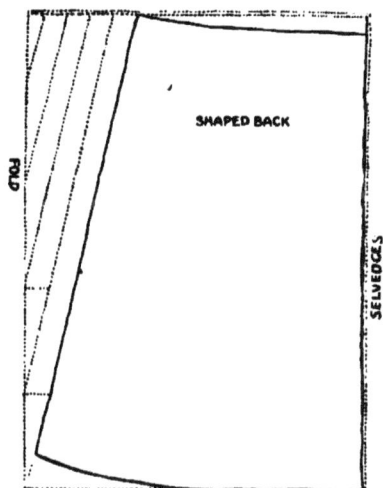

Diag. 84A.

The *skirt* should be cut out frequently in ordinary newspaper and memorized by the girl as the **Type**.

The straight edges must be placed to the slanting (bias) edges to prevent puckering and stretchiness, and should be machined as in previous lesson (French Seam), *or* counter-folded and machined first on one side and then on the other, *or* machined in two parallel rows on the right side (Diags. 60, 61, 62).

LESSON VII

WAISTBANDS AND FOOT FINISHINGS

AGE: 12–14 YEARS

SKIRT **Type** forms the base of this lesson.

Waistbands may be straight or shaped.

Method.—(1) A straight waistband consists in a strip cut selvedge wise, 1 inch to 2 inches in depth; doubled; top-sewn at the ends and hemmed or machined on to the gathered skirt or bodice (Diags. 85, 86).

(2) A shaped band may merely consist of strips, cut on the bias or cross, and joined together to form a false hem. This is placed to the edge of the skirt at the waist on the right side, machined, then turned over to the wrong side and machined on the right side along by the tacking stitch.

To avoid the doubling in of the cloth, it is advisable to machine a row at the top of the skirt.

Insert a draw string at the back from the seam next to the back one.

Diag. 85.

Diag. 86.

(3) Another way is to make a circular band. (This is incidentally the **Type** for the one-piece skirt.)

The band should be cut out first in ordinary newspaper. Take the length of waist rather loosely—say 24 inches. (One band and its lining can be cut out of ¾ yard.) Fold this length into two, selvedge wise, and from the top *folded* corner describe one quarter of a circle with the half length as radius. Measure in from the *open* top corner the depth of waistband, 4 inches to 5 inches, and describe a parallel curve (Diag. 87).

Slope sufficient, say from ¼ inch to ¾ inch, at the back of the band to allow for the spring of the back.

In narrowing or deepening the band, alter always by the bottom of the band.

Foot Finishings.—(1) By folding in the raw edges and hemming or machining. Note that all seams—sew and fell, run and fell, machining,

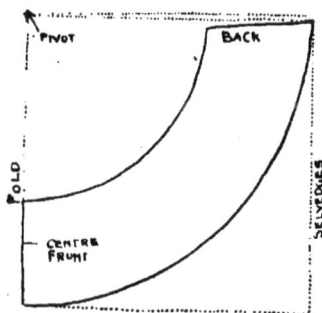

Diag. 87.

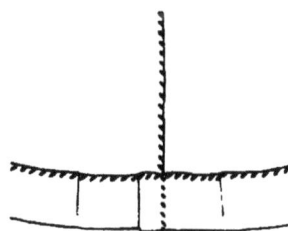

Diag. 88.

etc.—should match when folded over at *the end of seams*, and should not be pulled out of position on the inner side and sewn clumsily (Diag. 88).

(2) Straight foot bands are applied in exactly the same way as straight waistbands—hemmed, machined, or chain stitched, according to the purpose of the article made.

(3) Shaped flounces and frills form another method of finishing the end of seams in garments and household articles.

The principle is exactly the same as for the shaped circular waistband.

(4) Crossway bands and tucks.

LESSON VIII

EYELET HOLES—LOOPS—HOOKS AND EYES

AGE: 12-14 YEARS

As already suggested, the skirt may be fastened at the waist by a draw string.

This necessitates small holes for drawing through the string, known as eyelet holes.

Method.—Pierce the single material with a sharp-pointed round tool like a shoemaker's awl, and either top-sew very thickly or button-hole stitch the edges.

The button-hole knots should lie on the material and not at the edge (Diag. 89).

For hooks and lacing, the eyelet holes are worked through double material. The eyelet hole should be top-sewn in order that the hook may lie perfectly flat (Diag. 89A).

Eyelet loops are used with hooks and buttons.

Diag. 89.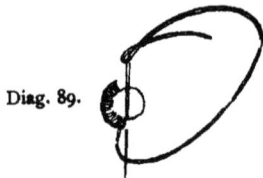Diag. 89A.

Diag. 90.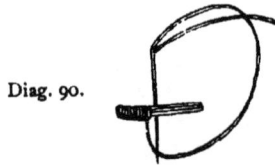Diag. 90A.

Four or five strands are sewn quite flat across the material for hooks (Diag. 90), or loosely at the edge of a band for buttons (Diag. 90A), and afterwards covered and strengthened with button-hole stitchery (Diag. 90A).

Eyelet holes can be practised as a simple decorative motif on the necks of chemises, etc. (Diags. 91, 67A).

. **Hooks and Eyes.**—These are made in different sizes: small for neckbands, medium for blouses, large for skirt waistbands. and garments made of thick material.

There is a quality called the "washing" hook, which though more expensive does not rust in washing. Ordinary hooks and eyes should not be used on washing fabrics, because of the iron mould stains.

Strong thread should be used; the rings and shanks top-sewn (Diag. 92).

When hooks and eyes are not covered with a facing, they should be button-holed instead of top-sewn.

Some prefer to have the entire edges covered to prevent any of the metal showing on the right side (Diag. 92).

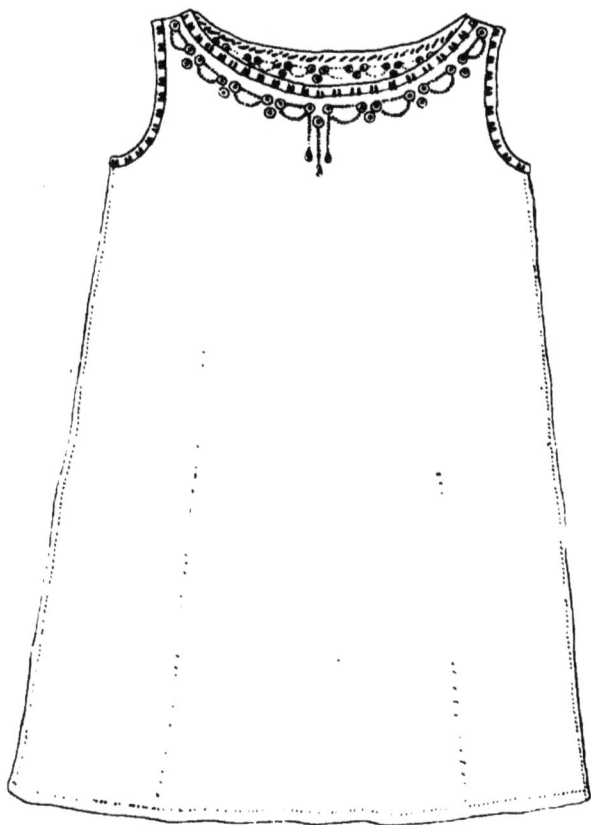

Diag. 91.   Diag. 92.

(Patent fasteners form a very popular method of fastening. They are small circular buttons, the convex structure of the one fits into the concave of the other very neatly. These are sewn on by strong hemming.)

LESSON IX

PATCHING—DARNING

AGE: 12-14 YEARS

THE *right feeling* which results from *following nature* through the primitive art period, conduces to that perception which includes **repair** in the architectural unity of construction and decoration.

Thus the intellectual fibre is prepared for the artisan period, and it behoves us to exercise and strengthen that fibre by a method of instruction which will give our girl or boy a sense of readiness in an emergency.

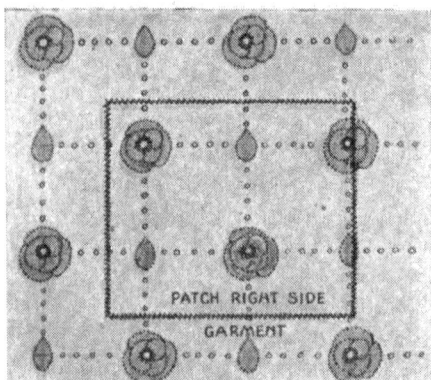

Diag. 93.

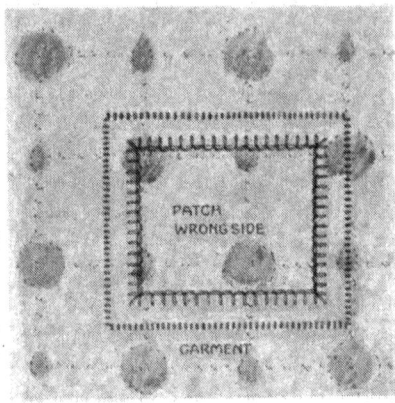

Diag. 94.

They should *see* many processes in many departments; *learn* something of the laws and principles that underlie all occupations, and know thoroughly one specific branch.

This can be accomplished in good measure by general repair lessons in needlecraft. Material—woollens, cottons, linens—have to be compared. (Incidentally the weekly habit of wardrobe inspection in relation to tidiness and the obviating of *large holes* insisted upon.)

Even when the child of the elementary school brings silk slips, lace slips, etc., part of the allowance of her charwoman mother—provided from the surplus of the rich man's house, the teacher finds that one principle holds good for all, *i.e.* repair should be as *unobtrusive* as possible with the requisite strength demanded by the article.

For example, thin materials—be they fine silk or fine lawn—should have—

(1) A fine needle ;
(2) A fine thread ;
(3) A fine stitch ;

and should therefore form the kind of repair suitable for classes after 14 years of age, when the hand becomes more and more skilful.

To lead to this nicety, it is with patching as with darning: *the understanding* of how to prepare carefully. One type of patch must precede the many varieties different holes suggest.

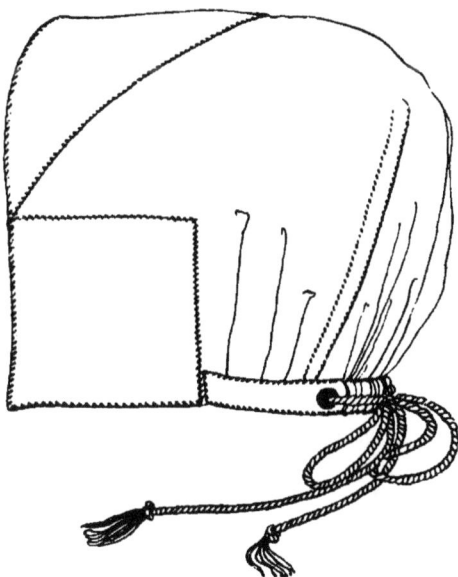

Diag. 95A.

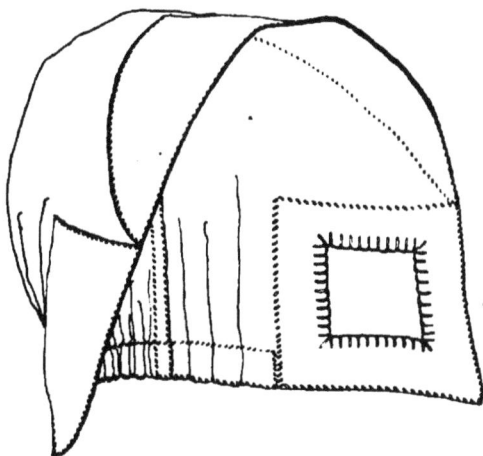

Diag. 95B.

Thick weight materials, such as serge, linen, cretonne, or medium . weights as prints, are treated alike because of *texture and pattern*.

Method.—The patch must match in pattern (for appearance) and warp (to avoid undue strain), and is placed on the right side with its opposite edges folded in for about ¼ inch, and top-sewed regularly and neatly to the article (Diag. 93).

The frayed edges on the wrong side are trimmed and button-hole stitched, about ¼ inch deep and ¼ inch apart (Diag. 94).

This can be practised on dust caps (Diags. 95 (A, B, C)), soiled linen bags, casement curtains, as a preparation for the actual hole.

Flannel is always patched down with herring-boning, using yarn or fine silk thread (Diags. 96A, 96B)).

All reversible cotton and silk fabrics have the patch placed *on the wrong side*, large enough to cover the surrounding worn area, and to allow for folds ⅛ inch to be turned in.

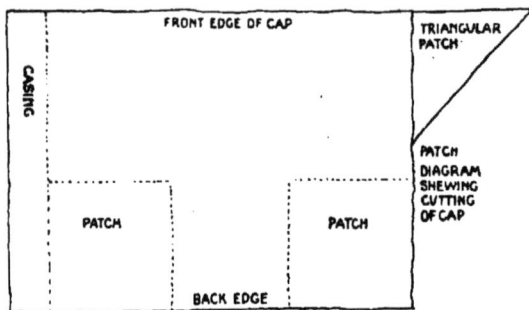

Diag. 95C.

The patch is pinned loosely, then the garment is turned to the right side, when all torn and frayed edges should be trimmed and a neat, economical, unobtrusive shape contrived. The square, oblong, triangular, or circular shapes should be placed on the wrong side, and in the very common tear (Diag. 97), where the garment is quite strong, but where a thin thread has given way resulting in a tear (possibly during washing or drying in the wind), it is wise to keep the existing shape and contrive a neat finish.

Calicoes and the fine fabrics already referred to should be top-sewed

Diag. 96A.

Diag. 96B.

on the right side and hemmed on the wrong (seams not wider than ⅛ inch (Diag. 97)).

But in all much worn material it is safe to note that patches hemmed on both right and wrong sides are enduring and pleasing.

Note the back of the dustcap (Diag. 95).

In an actual tear, due to nail or thorn or wind, nothing is neater than the edges sewn together by fish bone or German stitch—with thread corresponding to the material (Diag. 98). Occasionally a fine silk thread or single hair may be used successfully on thick woollens, alpacas, and tweeds—when the hand has gained skill.

In our approach to the ultili-tarian need, caps, etc. (Diag. 98A), may be made out of oddments, and these sewn together with a patch for the crown.

Special care is needed in patching a triangular piece of material, as the bias or cross-cut edge is apt to stretch very easily, and consequently the mending be-comes spoiled (Diag. 95).

Applying this method to the under arm, or knee of any garment, the portion at the seams should be unpicked, and the patches placed in separately at the two seam edges (Diag. 99).

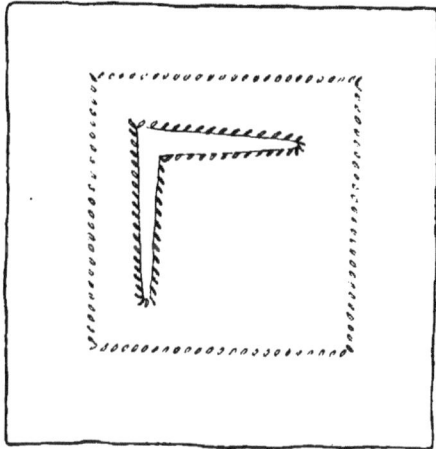

Diag. 97.

Complicated methods should be avoided, and the result that is quickly, securely, and economically accomplished, should be accepted.

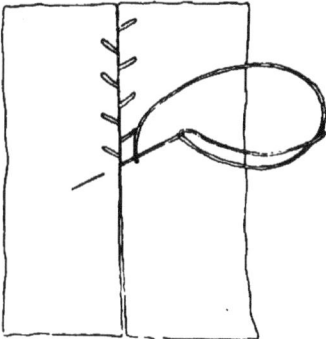

Diag. 98.

Diag. 98A.

In this way the girl is encouraged to act upon her own suggestion, and rely upon herself in matters of practical judgment.

F

Method.—**Darning.** The actual weaving or darning is now applied directly to the holed article, hand or machine knitted.

Darning needles are of long and medium sizes, and with eyes graded to suit fine cotton, silk and mending yarn, or five-ply fingering, as the texture demands, whether cotton, woollen, or silken goods.

It is of no consequence whether the darn be worked on the wrong or right side, as the weaving should be alike on both sides when regularly darned, and while it may look neater to have the loops on the inside, these shrink in after washing. With thread that has been washed and dried, there is no occasion to leave too much loop, merely work "easy,"

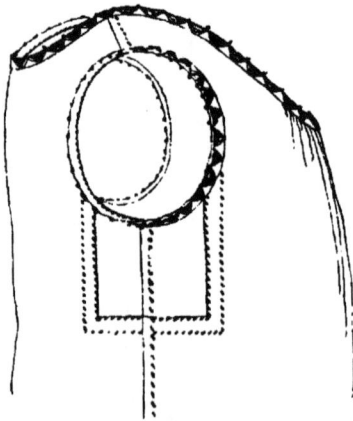 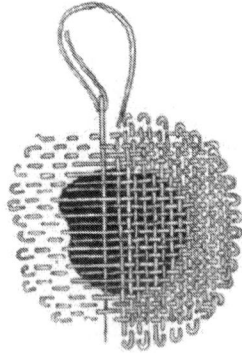

Diag. 99.   Diag. 100.

so that the elasticity of the knitting may be retained, and puckering, which occasionally appears after the first wash, be entirely prevented.

All ends and untidy edges should be trimmed : the *edges*, not loops, lifted with the needle at top and bottom alternately (Diag. 100) to keep the darn regular.

It is utterly impossible to fray out and lift the loops of machine-knitted articles.

And in darning finely woven articles, two threads may be lifted and passed alternately, because not only is a single fine thread tedious to darn with, it is much less comfortable to wear than a *two*-strand darn.

An irregular darn shape is best—the circle, for example (Diag. 100), as this divides the strain among many threads. Do not draw the thread tightly.

LESSON X

OPENINGS

AGE: 12–14 YEARS

THERE are many ways of arranging openings in garments and general household articles, and the worker should choose her method according to the *use* of the article. For uniformity in details of practice is not desirable, if it were attainable.

To say that any opening, or strip of material, be it *front, back, side,* or

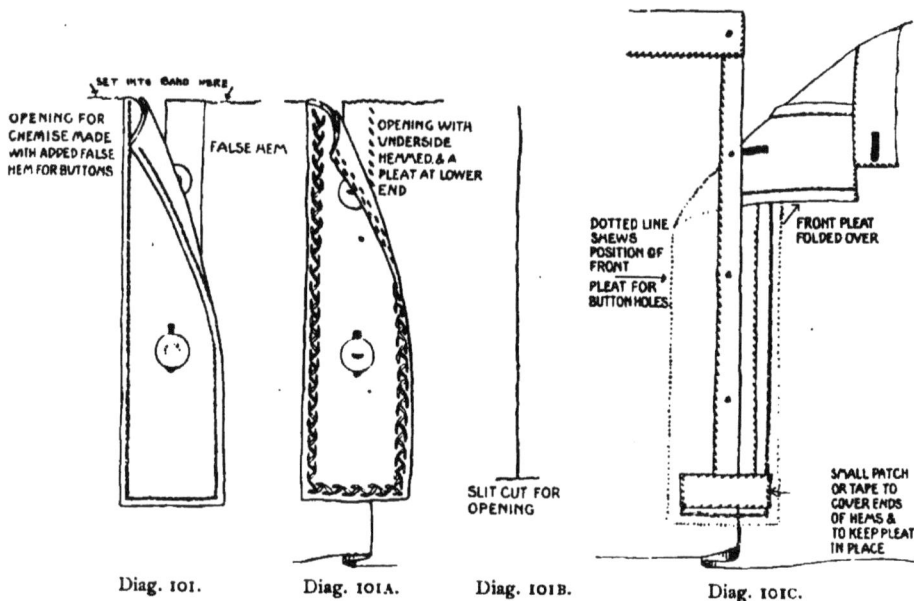

Diag. 101. Diag. 101A. Diag. 101B. Diag. 101C.

wrist, must be 3 inches, 13 inches, 23 inches, or the length of the garment, is on a par with saying that all are automatons, or do the same kind of work, are of one build, know no sickness; in other words, to work with our needle as if it bore no relation to the laws of health and comfort.

And since the days when men carried weapons of defence and found it easier to have the shirt opening fastening from left to right—women, with no such need, followed in this instance the more direct method, from which the rule stands even now, hence

　　Men's garments fasten left over right.

　　Women's garments fasten right over left.

　　Method.—Extra width of material may be allowed for all kinds of openings, finished like the slip bodice by simple folds hemmed. (1) An all-open front thus finished is approved of in many hospitals—nurses find

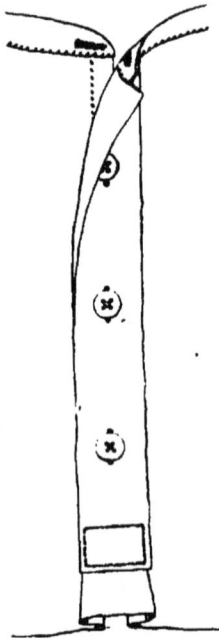

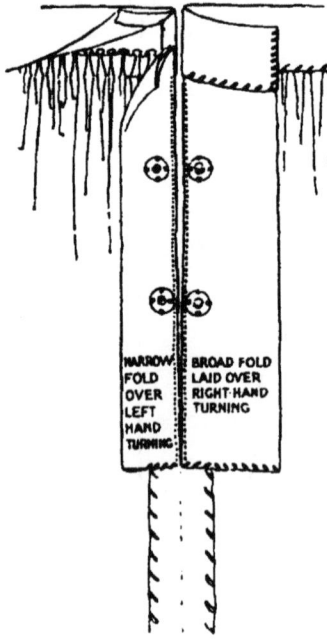

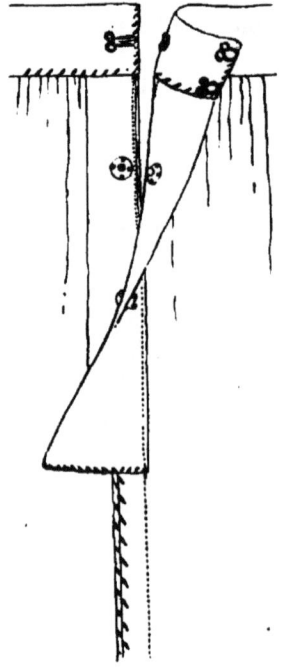

Diag. 102.　　　　　　Diag. 103.　　　　　　Diag. 103A.

the garments much easier to slip on and off, and the garment is saved from being unduly stretched or racked. (2) Without extra width of material, added strips may be placed on right and left sides respectively, singly as "false hems" hemmed or machined (Diags. 101, 101A), or double as "front, back, or side pleat"; fitting the purpose of the garment, as far as details of length and width apply.

　　For all, the same principle obtains.

　　Method.—Cut down the length decided on, snip at right angles

¼ inch to ¾ inch on either side, which allows the extra material at the foot of the opening to be formed into a pleat at the end of the band (Diag. 101B).

On the one side turn in a hem to the wrong side, or machine down a false hem (Diag. 101) (wide enough to hold a button comfortably). On the other side, place the strip (cut selvedge wise) on the wrong side of the garment.

At each end of this strip, leave extra material to allow (*a*) for the fitting of the neck curve; (*b*) for the particular finish at the other end— square, pointed, or rounded.

Machine or back stitch the two long edges ⅛ inch from the edge.

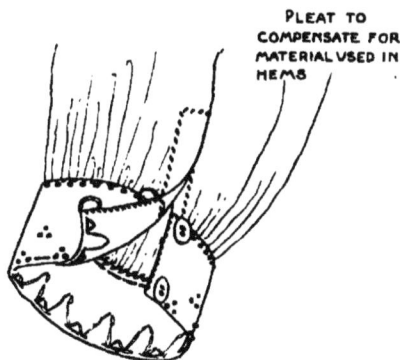

PLEAT TO COMPENSATE FOR MATERIAL USED IN HEMS

Diag. 104.

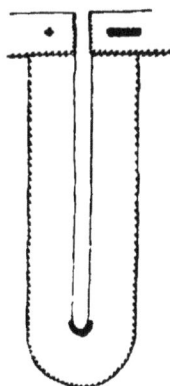

Diag. 105.

Flatten out and turn the strip over to the *right* side. Turn in the bottom edge of the band according to choice, and arrange the pleat by bringing the half of the band over the hem, so that the hem lies exactly under the middle of the band (Diag. 101A). Cover the ends of the hems with a small strip, hemmed neatly (Diag. 101C).

Stitch (by machining, chain stitching, or feathering) the band to the garment all round (Diags. 101, 101A).

Note that the extra material at the foot of the band may be box-pleated, as the custom is with a boy's or man's shirt (Diag. 102).

Diags. 103, 103A, 104, 105, illustrate various openings for sleeves, skirts, drawers.

LESSON XI

IN the graded types, leading up to 14 years of age, drawers, knickers, and all such divided garments come last, because they have been a later development of clothes in all civilizations, whether as trousers, pantaloons or pantelets.

Method.—(1) Best of all, start with a pilch (baby's drawers) (Diags. 106, 106A), where the garment is practically all seat and no leg.

This can be made out of one half-yard flannel, shaped very slightly for the leg, button-holed or bound; gathered and set in into a straight

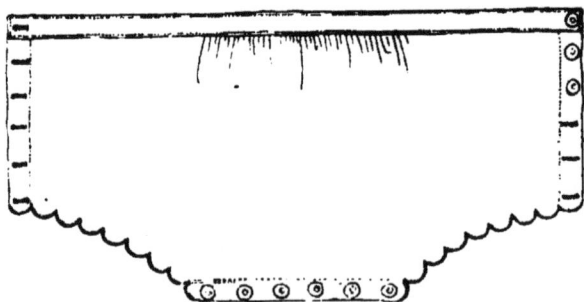

Diag. 106.

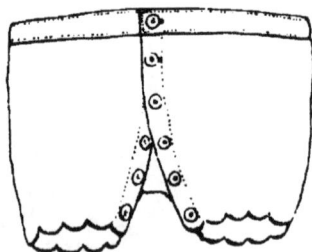

Diag. 106A.

waist band. Bands made of calico are less clumsy and do not shrink like flannel.

(2) Next take the child of six years, when the seat becomes a little less in proportion to the leg as it lengthens, *i.e.* three-quarters seat, approximately, to one-quarter leg (Diag. 107).

As the motion or action of the leg in relation to the proportion bears a similarity, three-quarters is allowed for the width of the leg (Diag. 107).

The middle of the back should be a little to the outside of the line drawn upwards from the leg width and gradually sloped down to the middle of the front to allow for the bending of the body.

The curve for the seat and the almost straight line across the front, finish the cutting out.

This may be made up in calico, nainsook, flannelette, wincey, union, flannel, etc.

Intelligence and the quality of alertness is stimulated and developed in this case by the girl having to note carefully—

(1) The pairing of right and left leg.

(2) The facing of seams.

(3) If the foot finishing have tucks, extra length must be allowed to each leg of the selected type.

(4) The type for the girl of fourteen years becomes still less in the seat, and consequently longer in the leg, *i.e.* two-thirds seat approximately to one-third leg.

Again remembering the anatomical similarity of proportion and motion, two-thirds is allowed for the width of the leg (Diag. 108).

The middle points, back and front, are decided as in the previous lesson, allowing gradually greater slope from the child period to the full-grown period.

The curves for the seat and the almost straight lines along the front are shaped as in the previous lesson.

(5) In the normal woman's size the seat and leg are equal in proportion, and as there is very little appreciable differ-

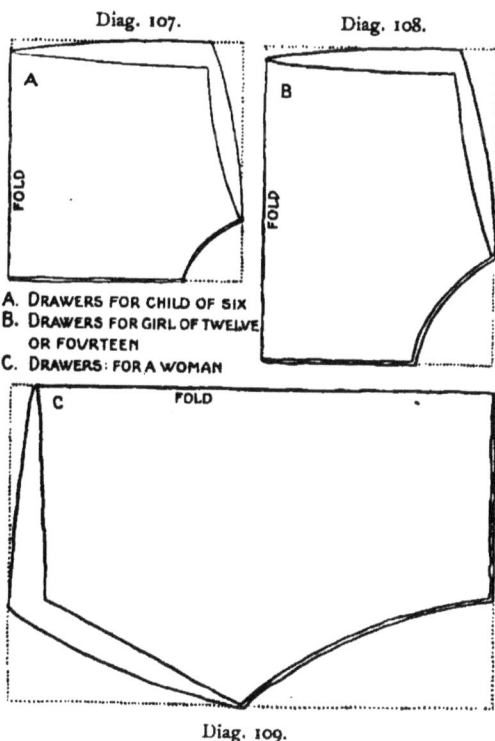

Diag. 107.

Diag. 108.

A. DRAWERS FOR CHILD OF SIX
B. DRAWERS FOR GIRL OF TWELVE OR FOURTEEN
C. DRAWERS: FOR A WOMAN

Diag. 109.

ence between the action of the 14-year-old girl and the adult, the width allowed for the action is the same in each type, *i.e.* two-thirds for the width of the leg.

Diag. 109. If a circular band be used, the depth of the band should be cut off the top of the paper pattern before cutting out in the material, to allow for the shaped band *going on*.

Diag. 110 illustrates the women's type *without* straight or shaped band, but fitted by means of darts, crossway strip and draw strings, at the waist, and by a flounce at the foot finishing, which may be simply

Diag. 110.

Diag. 111.

machined at the edge, gathered and set in, or decorated with one or other of the many kinds of stitchery now at the disposal of the girl.

Diag. 111 shows child's drawers buttoned to a bodice.

LESSON XII

SEWING ON OF LACE

AGE : 12–14 YEARS

LACE is ornament superimposed. It does not grow out of the structure ordinarily speaking. And to appreciate the simple, well-directed effort that results in honest, well-finished work, implies a muscular development of the eye which shows itself in the knowledge of beautiful form. This forbids bad ornament, or good ornament in the wrong place.

Strong, simple-patterned knitted lace used on household or personal belongings should be over-seamed. It is of no consequence whether this be done on right or wrong side (Diag. 112). Very fine or very narrow lace may be laid flat on the article and run (Diag. 113).

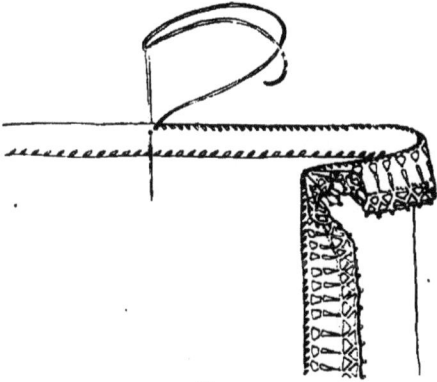

After the fourteenth year, when the consciousness of beauty impels to many devices, the expansion,

Diag. 112.

Diag. 113.

whether top sewn or run, must suit the purpose and the occasion.

Note that the beginnings and finishings are quite secure and neat.

LESSON XIII

YOKE, COLLAR-BANDS, WRISTBAND

Age : 12–14 Years

A yoke in relation to garments and household articles is a *support.*

Prehistorically, the covering of skin hung from a small support on each shoulder cut out of skin; this in time became woven—became a decorated shoulder emblem, and slowly expanded into circular, three-quarter, half supports or yokes, always being balanced in relation to the collar and collar-band.

And in .any renaissance movement in dress, this shoulder part has been seized to the modification or expansion of the purpose and use of the raiment.

The child should be led to see the meaning of the yoke as a support: and up to this point the teacher has forestalled the awakening by preparation through the graded **Types.**

Method.—Associate with slip bodice type and measure accordingly. The material used may be a contrast, or the same stuff as the rest of the garment. The yoke may be circular, as in the Child's Pinafore (Diags. 114, 114A, 114B), square as in the Woman's Blouse or Nightdress (Diag.

Diag. 114.

115). All such yokes cut in *one piece* shaped to fit the neck, shoulder and bust are termed saddle yokes.

Place the front of the paper pattern to the folded material if the garment is to have a back fastening; and if a front fastening, place the back of the paper pattern to the folded material. Cut out the neck

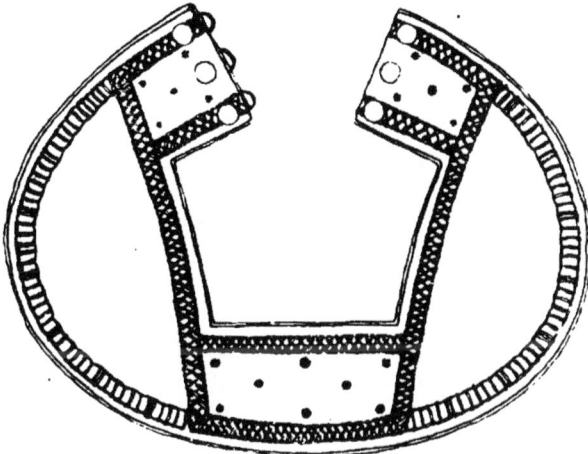

Diag. 114A.

curve, keeping fairly straight for
1 inch or 2 inches in the middle
of the back and front (Diag.
116). Note the relation between
shoulder and neck; cut down
front opening, bust line, and
shoulder curve.

Yokes may be cut exactly
like the slip bodice *with shoulder
seams*, but while more economical
with material this is less enduring for wear and tear. And as
most strain lies on the width
across the back, see that the
selvedge runs across. Material
may be gathered, stroked, and
set in to any yoke, or, if thick in
texture, pleated when used in
under garments requiring fre-
quent washing, or gauged (two
or three rows of gathers sewn
exactly parallel with about $\frac{1}{4}$ inch
between each row (Diag. 117).)

Diag. 114B.

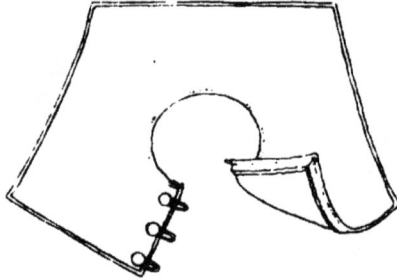

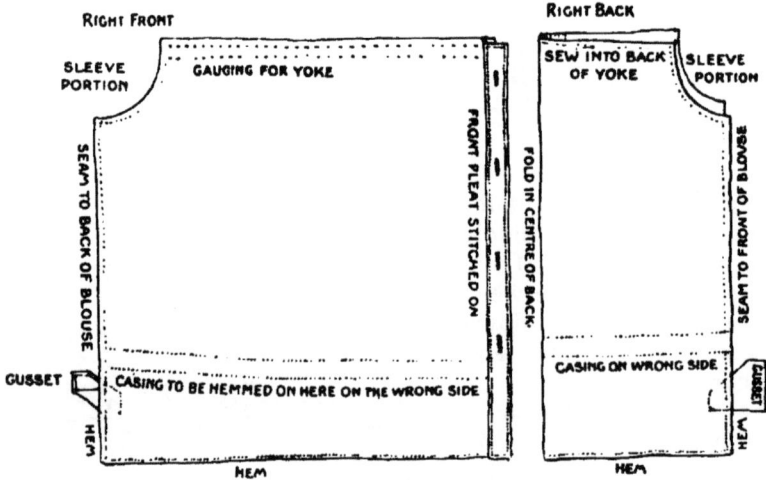

RIGHT FRONT

RIGHT BACK

SLEEVE PORTION

GAUGING FOR YOKE

SEW INTO BACK OF YOKE

SLEEVE PORTION

SEAM TO BACK OF BLOUSE

FRONT PLEAT STITCHED ON

FOLD IN CENTRE OF BACK

SEAM TO FRONT OF BLOUSE

GUSSET

CASING TO BE HEMMED ON HERE ON THE WRONG SIDE

CASING ON WRONG SIDE

GUSSET

HEM

HEM

HEM

HEM

Diag. 115.

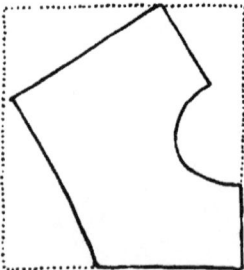

Diag. 116.

The neck may be finished

1. Without neckband.
2. Standing up band.
3. Lying down collar.

1. *Standing up bands.*

In boys' and men's garments two neckbands, length of neck plus $\frac{1}{4}$ inch to $\frac{3}{4}$ inch to allow for turnings and crossing over, are placed together, right sides facing. The ends and top edge are machined loosely to allow for shrinkage, then turned inside out and the shirt inserted between the two edges, and a row of machining done all round the collar (Diag. 122).

In chemises, or *nightdresses.*—A straight strip cut selvedge-wise 36 inches × 2 inches and doubled 36 inches × 1 inch should have the ends joined firmly and the opposite edges folded in ⅓ inch. Pin the band on

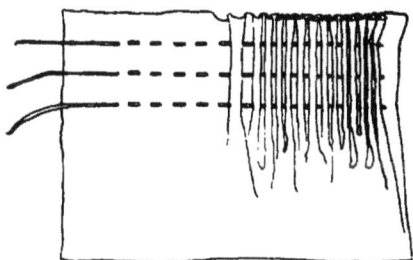

Diag. 117.

the shoulders of the chemise, allowing about 2 inches more to the front half of the chemise.

Note that the plain parts on either side of the shoulders be equally spaced. The band may be hemmed or machined all round on to the chemise, or finished by a front opening (Diag. 118).

Diagrams 119 and 119A illustrate blouse with high neckband finished with a piping and stitched.

(2) Lying down or turnover collars are shaped exactly like saddle yoke, rounded out the depth required, and either machined or hemmed into a narrow, straight band (Diags. 120, 121). Without a collar

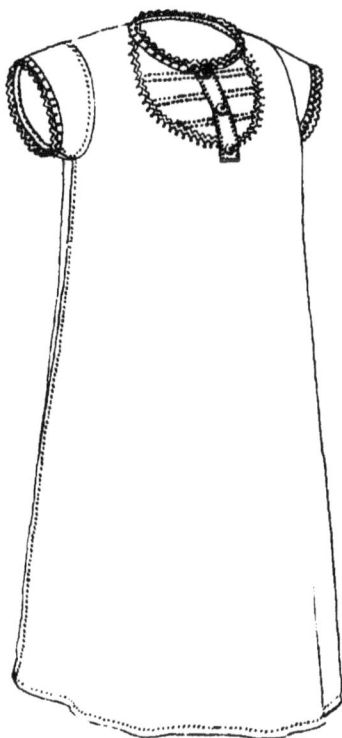

Diag. 118.

band, as for a man's nightshirt, the collar is stitched on to the yoke at back of the neck, and the front neck of the shirt is gathered up to fit (Diag. 122).

Wristbands.—Cuffs of all kinds should have the warp or selvedge threads lying lengthwise, as most strain occurs there in actual wear.

Wristbands or cuffs, whether straight or shaped, should be

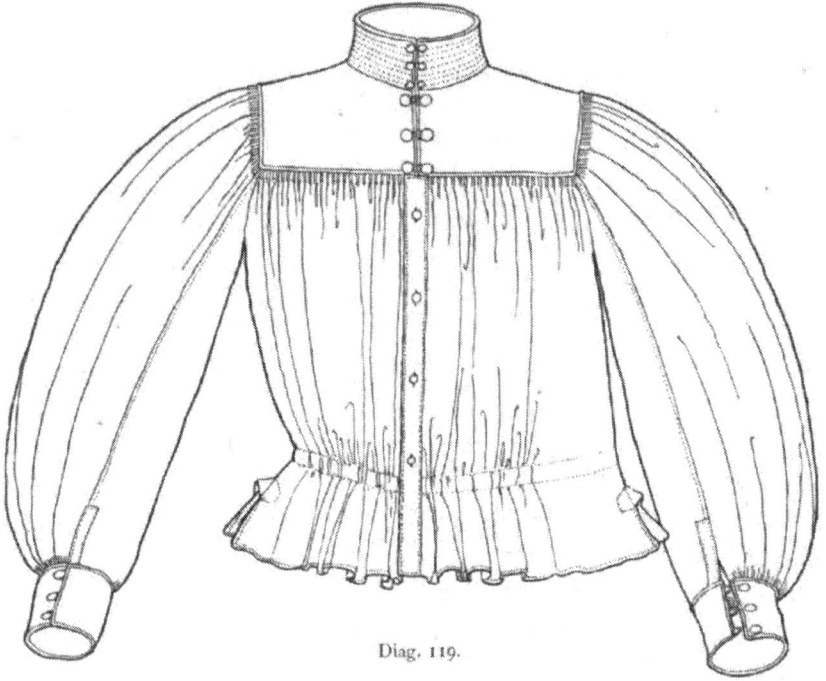

Diag. 119.

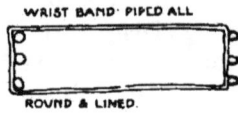

WRIST BAND· PIPED ALL
ROUND & LINED.

Diag. 119A.

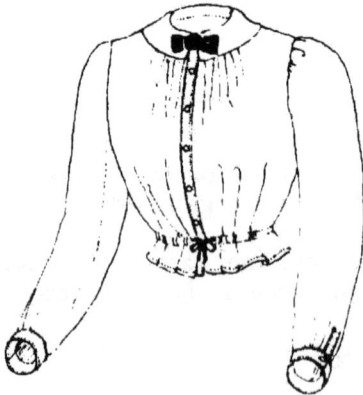

Diag. 120.

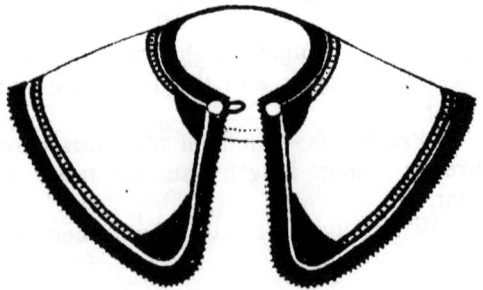

Diag. 121.

doubled and machined or sewn by suitable stitchery known to the girl.

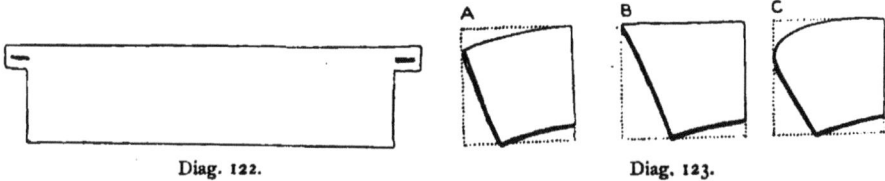

Diag. 122.   Diag. 123.

If shaped, the wrist measurement should be sloped up as in the sleeve type to suit the depth of cuff required (Diag. 123, A, B, c).

LESSON XIV

HOUSEHOLD ARTICLES : MARKING

AGE : 12-14 YEARS

TYPICAL household articles include pillow, bolster and mattress covers, sheets, coverlets, towels, tablecloths, serviettes, dusters.

Dusters, serviettes, plain towels are hemmed or machined with a rather loose stitch to allow for shrinkage.

A length of linen, double width, might be planned into towels, frayed out into fringed ends, overcast at the edges, darned and knotted into many pleasing varieties, either with cotton or white or ingrain flax (Diags. 124, 125). Instead of hemming the folds of tablecloths, these are often seamed for strength, and should have the fold at each end, like sheets, about ½ inch wide.

Circular calico is one of the products of the economic market which saves joining up the sides of bolster and pillow cases.

Bleached flour bags make very good serviceable coverings for pillows. Twill and linen last for years and always look well when laundried.

Marking is the term applied to the many varieties of sewing initials, full name, number, etc., on general personal and household equipment.

Chain stitch (known as French marking in the industrial world), fine tacking or darning, in fact, all the hitherto known stitchery, single and

combined, may be employed for marking.   Cross stitch is a time-
honoured method.   The stitch forms a series of diagonal crosses on the

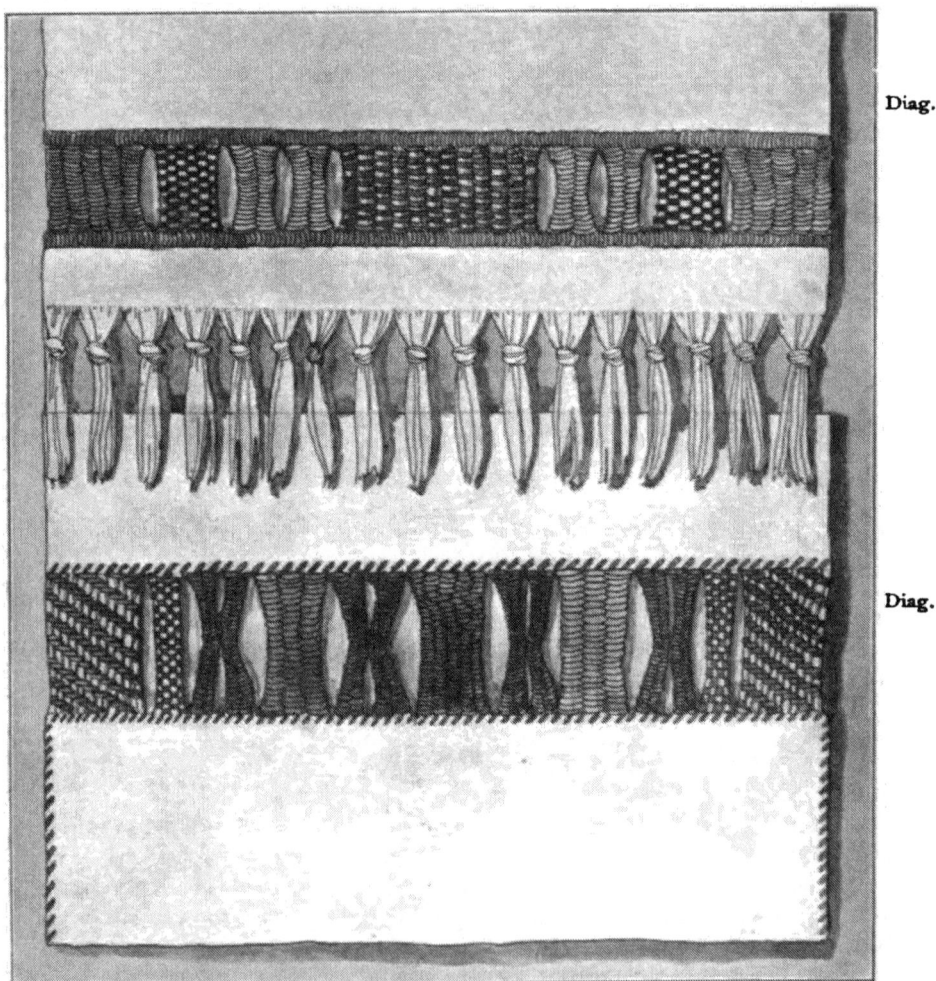

Diag.

Diag.

right side, and may be wrought exactly like top sewing, if one long row
is required—working the required number with half stitches and then

sewing back over each to form the cross (Diag. 126). Each cross complete in itself is sewn, however, by lifting as much on the needle as you pass over from the starting-place. Each cross complete in itself is worked from the starting-place by going down and across a few threads to the right, according to the thickness of the material, and lifting a few threads straight to the left (Diag. 127).

Bring the needle up and across a few threads to the right and so cross the first diagonal thread (Diag. 127).

Diag. 126.

For the second cross bring the needle up at the bottom right-hand corner of the first cross and continue as with the first cross. And in all cases leave the loose beginning thread to be sewn over with the cross-stitch thread.

The test of correctness is that the stitches should all cross in the same direction, *i.e.* either from right to left or left to right. Fasten off the thread by darning under and over the stitch and snip the thread end quite close to the lettering.

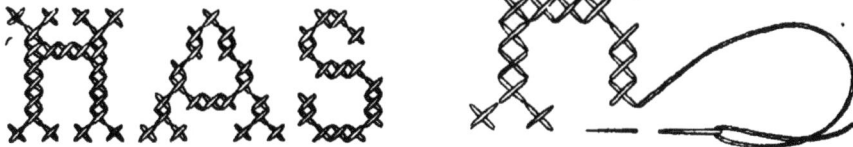

Diag. 127.

Note that each letter by any of the methods should be begun and finished by its own thread.

Eyelet holes make an interesting, decorative marking.

There are innumerable petty regulations as to the correct position for marking linen. It is best for the worker to consider carefully which will be the most convenient place to look for the marking and to place it there.

LESSON XV

THE MAKING OF SIMPLE PATTERN IN RELATION TO HOUSEHOLD ARTICLES AND
GARMENTS, WITH THE APPLICATION OF ANY OF THE PREVIOUS STITCHERY

AGE: 12–14 YEARS

(A)

IT is important that tidiness and an orderly habit of caring for garments, household equipment, etc., should characterize the girl.

Bags and cases for general mending lead to an orderliness in arranging drawers, trunks, etc.

A fairly large work-bag is necessary for the girl to hold the work for the repairing lesson. And this should be as simple and as beautiful as she can express.

Materials such as rough towelling, crash, sheeting, unbleached calico are all cheap and strong, and most suitable for this purpose.

Seams should be made an interesting feature; the girl can show her judgment in the construction and decoration of the bag.

The place likely to have most weight is the bottom—hence the mass of darning as simple motifs in Diag. 52 (see page 33).

This motif is repeated as small latchets for the strings, that in turn give a chance for the girl's *ingenuity* and *inventive* powers.

One half-yard of rough towelling costs 2*d*. to 3*d*.: mending yarn, cotton embroidery and unbleached tape, strings or cords of their own making. The bag costs 6*d*., but bleached flour bags at 2*d*. each work out about 4*d*. per child, counting thread, etc.

(B)

Simple cushions in similar material to the work-bag give opportunity to the pattern-making instinct to express itself usefully and beautifully through the stitchery already known.

Diag. 128 shows a pincushion, spaced fittingly for pins—its purpose, weighted at the corners, and connected by a few lines of decoration.

Experimental work shows varied and interesting patterns, which later, as in an earlier stage, becomes part and parcel of the structure.

This care of personal and household belongings, means nicety of taste, that *right feeling* which in itself is an emotion working to healthful, beautiful ends. In our advancing civilization the useful *alone* is no more to be our aim and end than is the mud dwelling of the mound dweller,

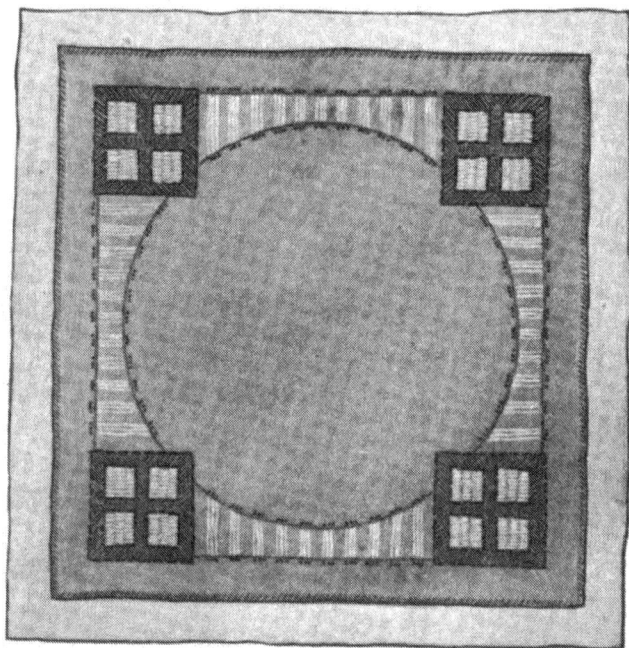

Diag. 128.

or the square cavity in the brick wall to be the aim of the architect who can plan also " The lancet arch or the glowing and melting harmony of gold and azure."

SECTION III

AGE: 14–18 YEARS.   AGE: 18–24 YEARS

LESSON I

EXPANSION OF COMBINED TYPES INTO NIGHTDRESS, OVERALL, WRAPPER, ETC.

AT 14 years of age, the girl enters a fresh period of life.

The brooding, slack time is over. Nerve cells hitherto sleeping awaken, and immediately the higher cerebral regions show, amongst other characteristics, *a consciousness of beauty.*

Now, this consciousness of

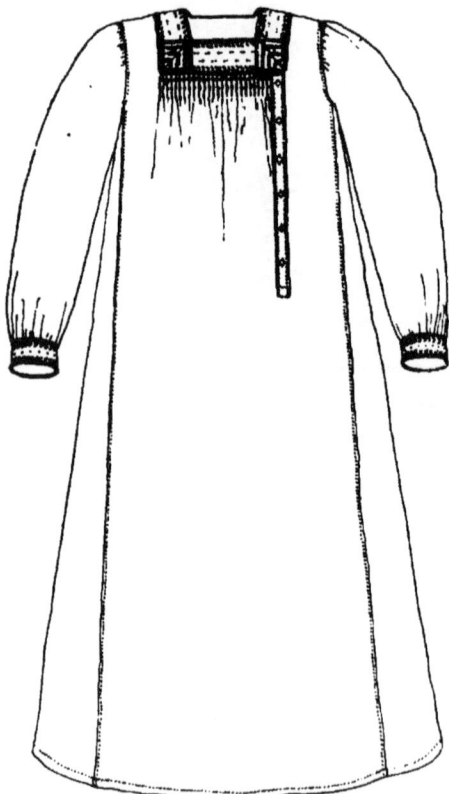

Diag. 129.

Diag. 130A.

beauty should be directed and embodied through beautiful, stimulating, but *hard* work.

Colours of material and thread give beauty and stimulus: the

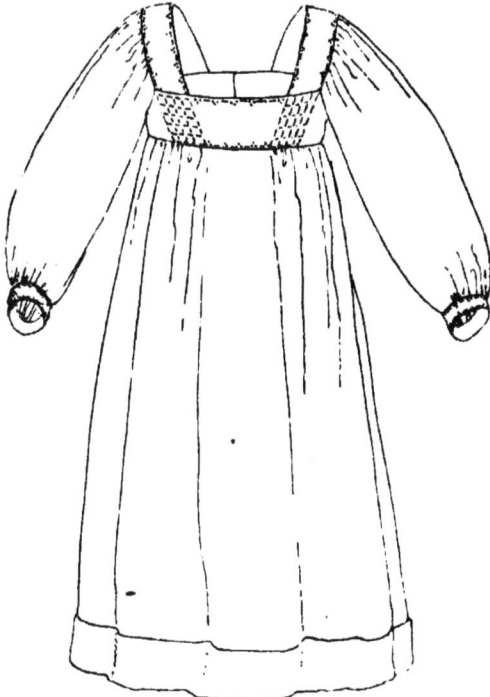

Diag. 130B.

Diag. 131.

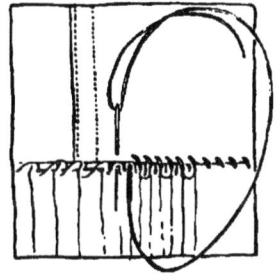

Diag. 132.

expansion of stitchery and the more complex construction adapted to the growing mind give the hard work.

As the social wisdom of the book appeals likewise to the awakening mind, it is advisable not to repress rapid growth by slighting this or that magazine of fashion and opinion selected by the adolescent, but rather encourage frank expression of interest and a searching spirit for what is good in any or all.

The nightdress (Diag. 129) shows the slip bodice, sleeve and skirt types modified here, expanded there; but with the types intelligently learnt, the opportunity for the variations is welcomed by our adolescent. Note the decorative and constructive quality of the stitchery at the corners of the square yoke.

Diag. 133.

The overalls (Diags. 130A and 130B) show differences in construction, resembling the experimental work done by the girl at this period.

The wrapper or housemaid's dress (Diag. 131) follows fairly closely the three elementary types (slip bodice, sleeve, skirt). The skirt may be gathered or pleated into the band, or guaged and top-sewed into the waistband (Diag. 132).

Diag. 134.

The girl's pinafore dress (Diag. 133) illustrates as well as the sleeveless bodice (Diags. 134, 135), the consciousness of beauty embodied in simple forms.

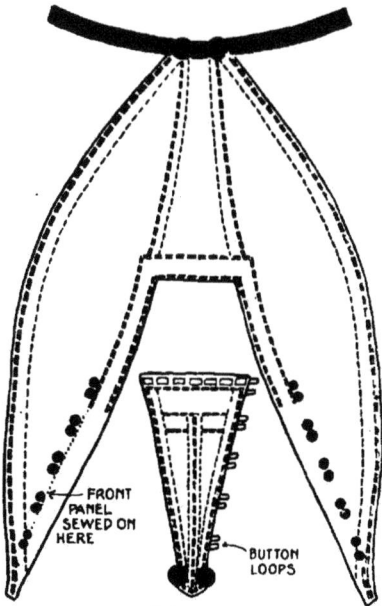

FRONT PANEL SEWED ON HERE

BUTTON LOOPS

Diag. 135.

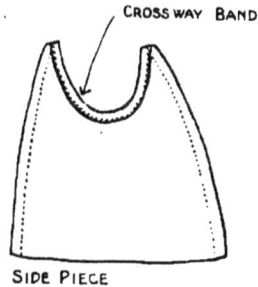

CROSSWAY BAND

SIDE PIECE

LESSON II

AGE: 14–18 YEARS

Couching is a stitch *par excellence* suited to pile fabrics (velvet, velveteen) or to thick woollen materials, the surface of which does not readily adapt itself to accurate placing of the needle, and which is difficult to mark with pattern. On such materials, the main lines of the pattern may be defined by a thick thread or some strands of thread laid on the line, and sewn with about 6 or 7 stitches to the inch, so that the over-seam stitch may lie at right angles to the couching thread. After this the smaller details of the embroidery may be worked in with other stitches if these are desired (Diag. 136).

Snail Trail is an excellent stitch for the rapid working of lines, and is suitable for any firm material. It also makes good filling for large spaces

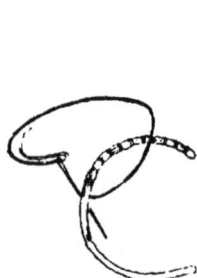
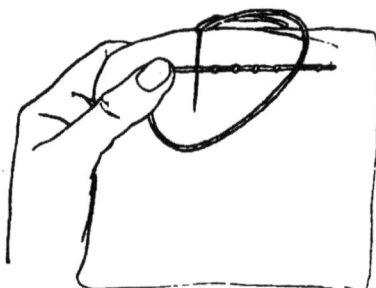

Diag. 136.   Diag. 137.   Diag. 138.

worked close together in lines. It is equivalent to couching worked with one thread (Diag. 137).

Hold the thread down about one inch from where it comes out with the left thumb. Place the needle vertically close above the thread and bring it out again through the loop immediately below the thread, thus forming a knot—the knots to be placed from $\frac{1}{4}$ to $\frac{1}{2}$ inch apart, according to the thickness of the thread used.

Twisted Chain Stitch is worked much like the last, but the line of stitches is worked vertically as in chain stitch, and the knots are larger, and are worked close together (Diag. 138). This stitch must be worked loosely, and is best suited for soft materials.

Outline Stitch.—A line of slightly sloping stitches worked from left to right, each stitch commencing about the middle of its predecessor (Diag. 139). Suitable for all smooth materials.

Feather Stitch.—This is a variant of button-hole stitch, worked vertically from top to bottom ; the looped stitch is worked zigzag fashion, first to left of the line, and next a little lower diagonally to the right of it. The needle may take up its stitches either diagonally or vertically, as the

| Diag. 139. | Diag. 140. | Diag. 141. | Diag. 142. |

imagination of the worker dictates, and the zigzags may be composed of either one or more stitches to left and right in regular sequence, as in Diags. 140, 141. This stitch is best suited as a trimming for washing garments.

⌠ **Double Chain Stitch.**—An expansion of feather stitch. The needle is set in vertically immediately below the loop of the stitch above—producing a braid-like appearance (Diag. 142).

Braid Stitch.—This is an excellent stitch for making raised lines or stems in wool or linen thread.

A long diagonal stitch is made from left to right downwards, the needle then directed through the

Diag. 143.

material horizontally from right to left, coming out below the commencement of the first stitch. The thread is then taken upwards diagonally rather above the end of the first diagonal stitch, making a slightly less sloping stitch than the first and in the opposite direction. Repeating this process forms a beautiful plaited appearance, which may be from $\frac{1}{8}$ to $\frac{1}{2}$ inch wide (Diag. 143).

Hem Stitching.—This is suited for linen material, where the warp and weft are even in thickness and strong enough to be easily withdrawn without breaking the threads. It is especially used as an adornment for hems.

Leave the required width of material for the hem and its turnings and draw out a sufficient number of threads to gather up without puckering, more or less according to the thickness of material, say from five to ten threads; then tack the folds of the hem into place, and with a thread of suitable thickness and colour take a stitch out of the right-hand end of the hem beneath four or five of the drawn threads towards the left (Diag. 144A). Take the needle back to where it was inserted under the drawn threads and set it under them again diagonally, so that the point comes out at the edge of the hem, as in 144B, thus gathering the drawn threads into little sheaf-like bundles by a loop. The other edge of the drawn threads may be stitched in the same fashion, the stitches either corresponding with the row along the hem, or by alternating with them

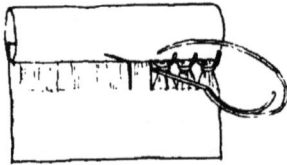 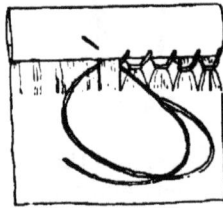 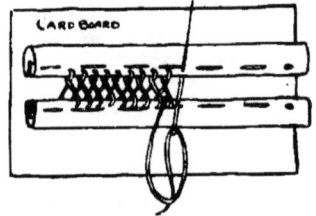

Diag. 144A.　　　　Diag. 144B.　　　　Diag. 145A.

so as to divide the sheaves of drawn threads and forming thus a zigzag arrangement.

Faggot Stitching.—This is chiefly used as a trimming for blouses and other garments of thin material, where it is desirable that one or more bands of material be fastened together by lacy open work.

Take a narrow strip of cross-cut lawn or similar material about 1 inch wide and fold both edges inwards, forming a narrow band about ⅓ to ½ inch wide. Tack this in a straight or curved line, as the required shaping demands, to a firm piece of cardboard, taking care not to pull out the material too tight. Then lay the hem of the material to be trimmed (or a corresponding band) parallel to the first and tack to the cardboard.

The stitch is a variant of herring-boning, but the needle is inserted close to the folded edge of the band vertically, forming loops (instead of horizontal stitches) on the wrong side (Diag. 145A).

If many bands are required to be shaped, for instance, into a neckband, it is advisable to draw the shape out on the cardboard and to tack the bands into place along both edges (Diag. 145B).

Smocking.—This is a form of decoration best suited to thin woollens,

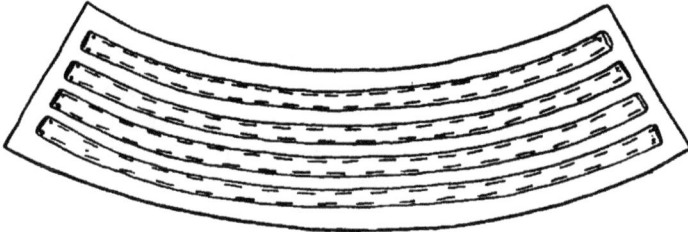

Diag. 145B.

cottons, silk or linen, and is chiefly used as a means of finishing children's dresses and shirts where much fulness is desired. Carefully gather up the portion of the garment to be smocked with rows of very regular gauging at intervals of $\frac{1}{2}$ to $\frac{3}{4}$ of an inch, and fasten the ends of the

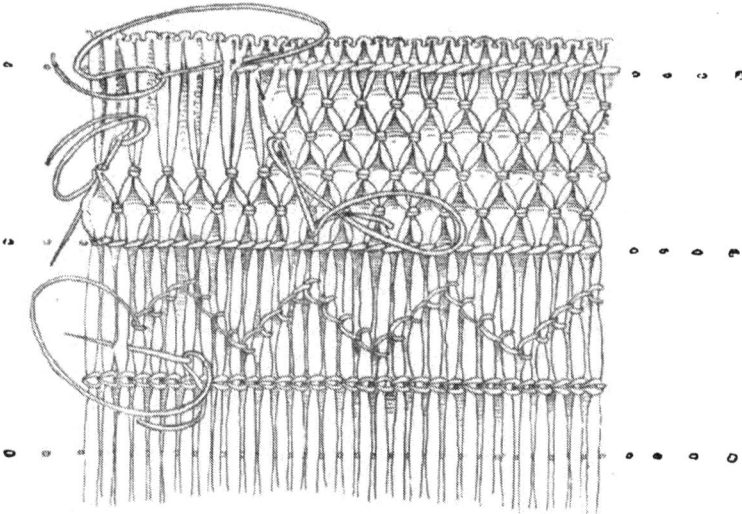

Diag. 146.

gauging threads to pins after drawing them to the required width. Diagram 146 shows some of the various stitches commonly used in smocking. The first is a row of outline stitch, taking up two folds of the material at a time.   Care must be taken not to make this stitching too tight.   Next comes **Honeycomb Stitch** where two folds of the material are caught together by two small firm stitches, and the needle is then directed along underneath one of the folds about half an inch, brought out there, and this fold and the next in succession caught together in like manner to the first pair, the folds have thus a zigzag direction given to them between the upper and lower rows of stitches.   Many rows of this stitchery give a honeycombed appearance to the material, but great care is necessary to keep the rows of stitches perfectly even.

Feather stitching and chain stitching may also be employed, each stitch taking up one single fold of the gauging.   When finished the first gauging threads may be withdrawn.

Satin Stitch.—This is merely top sewing laid out flat and the stitches set close together.   It is perhaps the most commonly used stitch in embroidery, and is suited for practically all materials, save when the pile is deep, and then it must be used inside an outline of couching or other similar stitch.   If a certain modelled or raised effect be desired, as in white embroidery, it is advisable to pad the surface which is to be satin stitched with several long stitches of coarse thread, which may then be covered over.

In such things as leaves or other forms where veins or lines of drawing must be carefully kept, the worker may define these by making them the junction between one set of stitches and another.   Care must always be taken not to work one set of satin stitches into another, as this gives a ragged or indefinite appearance to the work.   Diags. 147, 148 and 149 give examples of this stitch.

Diag. 150 illustrates **Long and Short Stitch**, which is a method of satin stitching best adapted for working one colour gradually into another, as in the shaded petals of flowers.

Diag. 151 illustrates **Oriental Stitch**, where a long stitch is taken horizontally from left to right of the space to be covered, the needle is then brought out close above this long stitch, a little inside of the outline, and is then inserted just below the long stitch near its other end, thus making a long diagonal stitch across the first which pins it down and which is peculiarly suitable for covering large spaces.   This stitch is best adapted to work on wool, arras, or linen.   If very large spaces are to be filled in, *two* diagonal stitches may be made across the long one (Diag. 152).   Another variety of this stitch is well suited for veining leaves, and here the needle is brought out above the very centre of the long stitch and inserted immediately below it (Diag. 153).

Shadow Stitching.—A method best suited to working on muslin or other transparent fabrics, is merely herring-boning stitched closely together on the *wrong* side of the material, so that it gives on the right side a neat outline of small stitches with a padded appearance on the

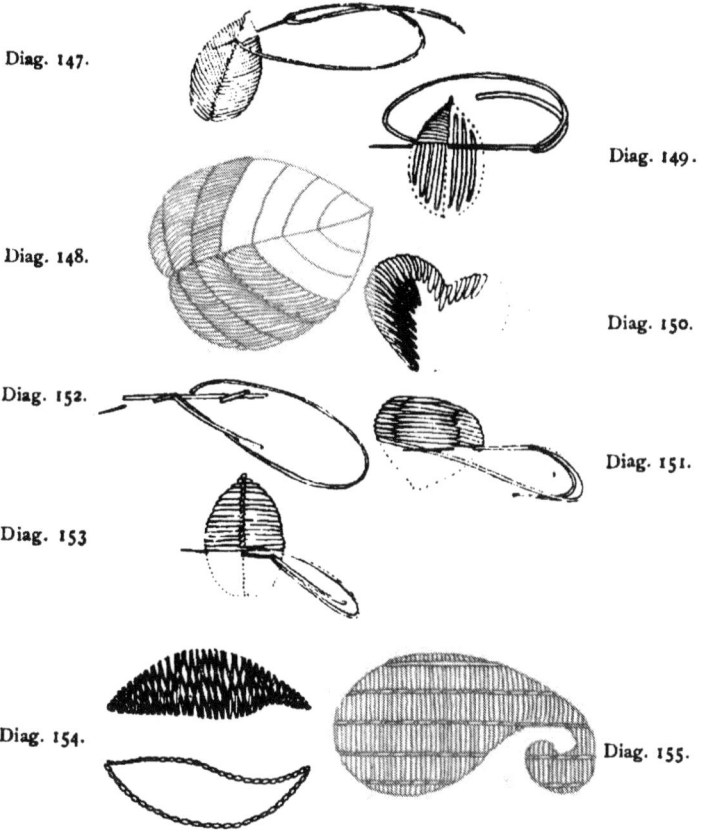

Diag. 147.

Diag. 149.

Diag. 148.

Diag. 150.

Diag. 152.

Diag. 151.

Diag. 153

Diag. 154.

Diag. 155.

surface enclosed by them. Diag. 154 shows the wrong and right side of a leaf worked thus.

Laid Stitch (Italian or Arabian Stitch) is a beautiful method of filling large surfaces on firm materials ; this stitch is best done on a frame, and is particularly suited for working in gold or tinsel threads, wool or flax, or coarse silk. The surface to be worked is covered first with long parallel stitches close together, and these are crossed later at intervals by others at right angles to them, spaced wide apart, $\frac{1}{2}$ inch to 1 inch, which are again couched down by a finer thread (Diag. 155).

LESSON III

EXPANSION OF TYPES INTO KNICKERS, COMBINATIONS, WHIPPING ON A FRILL

AGE: 14–18 YEARS; 18–24 YEARS

THE expansion of the drawers type into knickers shows the application of a shaped (circular) waistband. Any fulness in front is disposed of by darts.

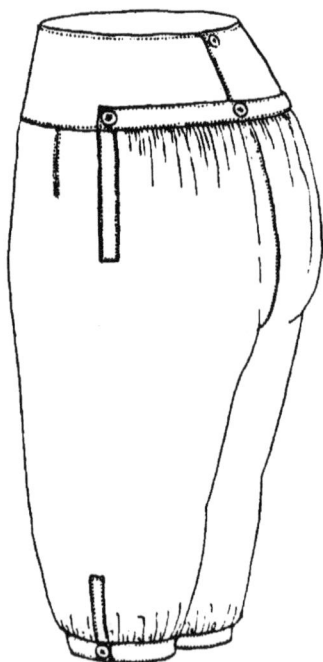

Diag. 156.

The upper portion of the back is gathered (pleated if in thick material) into a straight band and fastened to the circular band by buttons and button-holes (Diag. 156).

Side openings at waist and knee are finished as described already.

It is advisable to make up from the simple drawers type two or three movable slips (lining) or washing material, in fact, worn calico nightdresses, calico combinations or calico knickers might be adapted economically for this purpose, to wear with cloth knickers. These have taken the place of the *under* flannel petticoat to a great extent, and are to be recommended, being warmer, more comfortable, and quite as hygienic. In making up, the machine may be used for all seams.

Combinations combine the slip bodice and drawers type, and are certainly more economical than two separate garments.

But combinations of calico, etc., have neither the *elasticity* nor *warmth* that knitted combinations possess, and are not recommended for children or old people.

Combinations are made from $2\frac{1}{2}$ to 3 yards (adult size), and are made up by the processes employed already in the slip bodice and drawers types.

Note that the upper part of the seat is gathered and attached to the lower part of the bodice back.

The darts at the waist line should not be cut until all else is com-

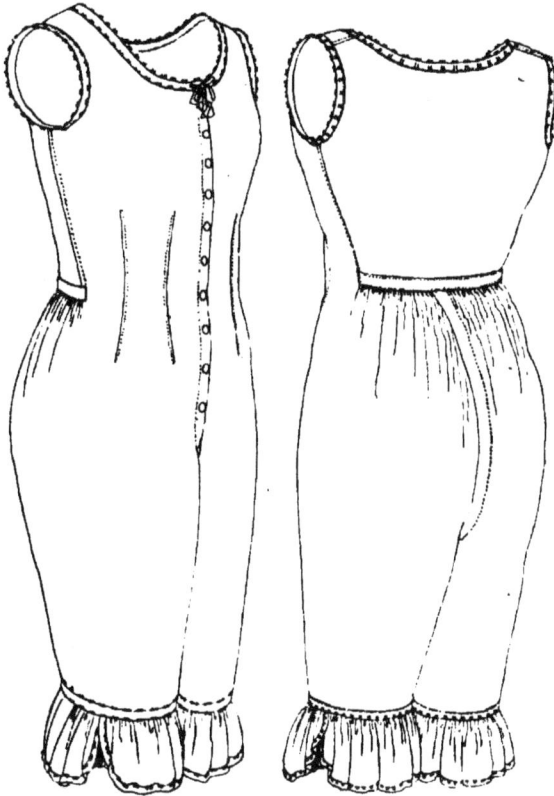

Diag. 157.

pleted, and then they should be sewn to match the other seams (Diag. 157).

Neck, armholes, kneebands may be constructed and decorated at the same time by the application of some of the varied stitchery known now; or a whipped frill may be sewn on as a finish.

For the general making up the machine may be used.

Whipping and sewing on a frill require growth and skill of hand, for fine material—be it fine calico, linen, or silk—has to be handled in small quantities. Much handling creases and depreciates the symmetry of the frill, which should follow the principles of gathering, stroking, setting in. Folds, if hemmed or machined, should be narrow, to avoid the bulging induced by gathering up deeply folded material that has not been constructed by suitable stitchery. The frill on the combinations shows vertical hemming grouped and varied by small tacking or darning stitchery.

The whipping stitch is worked from right to left, beginning with two or three hemming stitches.

Roll three-quarters of an inch at a time towards the worker, moving the raw edge backwards and forwards with the thumb over the left forefinger, which should be kept pretty motionless, till a tight roll is secured.

Move (whip) the needle from the back to the front in a slanting direction clear under the roll, with about ⅛ inch space between each whip, stitch and keep the thread quite easy (Diag. 158.) Test the work by drawing the material up every three-quarter inch. (If the needle come through the roll it is fatal, as the frill will not draw up and the thread breaks.)

Place the right side of the whipped-up frill to the right side of the garment and arrange the fulness equally all round with pins. Seam the frill (fulness) to the garment from the wrong side; the needle is inserted in a slanting direction, and lifts lightly the top of each separate whipped-up roll (Diag. 159), and the thread falls regularly between each of the rolls made.

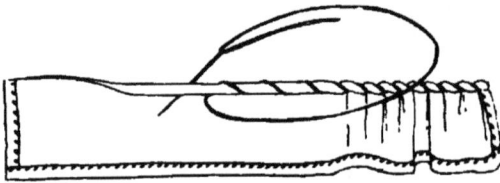
Diag. 158.

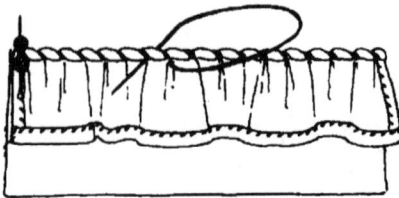
Diag. 159.

Paper patterns are presented free by many papers; patterns are bought for a trifle, but with one and all it is better to compare the pattern with the body, to see if all is correct, and if it be a fairly tight-fitting garment like the combinations, it is a safe plan to cut out the pattern in cheap, unbleached calico, *as the slip bodice type was cut out*, and fit this to the body.

Note, the neck and armhole in bought patterns are generally larger than required, and look carefully whether turnings have been allowed for, or not.

Before cutting out in the actual fabric, be sure that the pattern is placed rightly with regard to the way of the selvedge and those parts that have to face (blouses, shirts).

Skirt patterns, if too long, should not be shortened either at top or foot, but should have a tuck or two run at a sufficient distance from the foot, not to interfere with the important lines of the pattern.

If the pattern be too short, insert a piece of paper a similar distance from the foot edge. Gores are widened in a similar manner. In fitting take up at the shoulder seams or let out at the seam under the arms.

The baby's cap (Diag. 160) illustrates material whipped and set into a small crown of button-hole stitchery and eyelet holes.

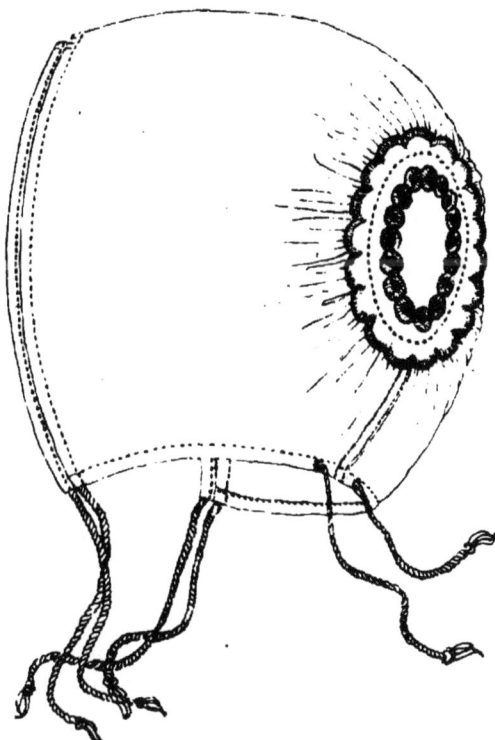

Diag. 160.

LESSON IV

BEGINNINGS OF PATTERN

AGE: 14–18 YEARS; 18–24 YEARS

ON looking back at the first lessons in this book it will be immediately evident that any recurrent stitches, or groups of stitches, in orderly arrangement resolves itself into *Pattern*, and the making of such pattern in

H

the construction of seams and of hems on garments or household gear is one of the most primitive developments of artistic decoration in civilization—in fact, it is frequently the first, and almost the only, civilized trait among certain barbaric peoples. Now, design in its broadest sense may be either decorative or it may confine itself to bare utility with no hint of beauty about it. Design is, in fact, *any* work that is not accidental, but in the sense in which it is generally used as "**Applied Design,**" it signified an intentional combination of utility with more or less of ornament, and is specially used in connection with what are called "Applied Arts." Design should in its elements be applied, first of all, to adorn and strengthen the construction of those things we work at. In architecture, in making of furniture, in the construction of everything we use in our houses, the value of the work is increased tenfold if this quality of Beauty be combined with its form.

There seems no reason why, if it do not combat with the utility of the work, we should not make ornament of our hems and seams far more than we do. Surely we have no reason to be ashamed of them! And if this structural design were insisted upon, there would be less need for the application of trimmings such as lace and complicated braiding which, unless it be of the most expensive, is unprofitable to wear, and now that we have learned the general application of stitchery we may make use of the sewing machine for long seams, and expand our hearts and our handiwork in adding ornament and beauty to such parts of our garments as may be most enhanced by them.

In making ornament of embroidery for garments or for useful household articles, it is important to avoid any too pictorial or naturalistic representation of floral or other forms.

If *pictures* are designed it is essentially *not* on our clothing, and paint and paper or canvas are the right mediums for such illustrative work. On our garments and on most textile fabrics we want Pattern—not Pictures, and a pattern is built up in an entirely different fashion from a picture. If we take two letters of the alphabet, for instance, or even only one, what delightful letter borders they can make if we will only be contented to use such simple motives without the foolish idea that this is too easy a thing to call "design," and we must cram it up with more complications in order to show people what we can do!

We take the letter O, for instance, and perhaps a "full stop." Well, we can all write, though we cannot all draw much, so of Os and full stops let us make a design. We can plan it out with a ruler, or on squared exercise paper, if we like (Diags. 161, 162). Or take a G and an M, and we have quite a pretty border design, and one that can turn a corner quite neatly too (Diag. 163). We can make good pattern out of any single shape, but in its beginnings it is best to keep to more or less geometrical forms and to apply our ingenuity to seeing how many different things we can make of them. This Creative Faculty has been sadly starved in many of us, for our education has tended more to direct our attention to the interpretation of other people's ideas, rather than to the development of our own individual ones, and the possibilities for bringing them out ; and

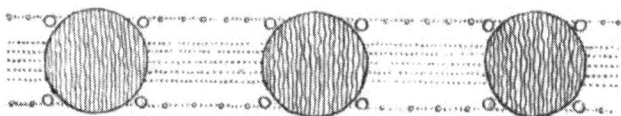

Diag. 161.

Diag. 162.

Diag. 163.

it is probable that, were greater scope given to the inventive powers of our children, we should find a vast number of new and useful ideas develop-ing, since no two men, women, or children have ideas exactly alike. The work of the hand in construction and invention demands all our reason-ing powers : the eye must balance, proportion, and measure with accuracy ; the mind must consider the strength of the material to resist tension, and wear and tear, the suitability of the work for its ultimate use. Harmony of colour, beauty of form, poetry of symbolism, even these can all be contained in the simplest design worked with a needle and thread, so that many branches of study, mathematics in particular, are represented in the design a girl may make in her clothing or other stitchery, if she be permitted to exercise her powers rightly upon its invention.

LESSON V

DESIGNING WITH STRAIGHT LINES

Age: 14–18 Years; 18–24 Years

Border patterns are the best suited for the designer as the preliminary exercises in planning embroidered decoration, and at first all such decoration should be made with a ruler on *straight* lines only, vertical or horizontal. Squared paper may be used as a convenience in measuring.

Diag. 164.

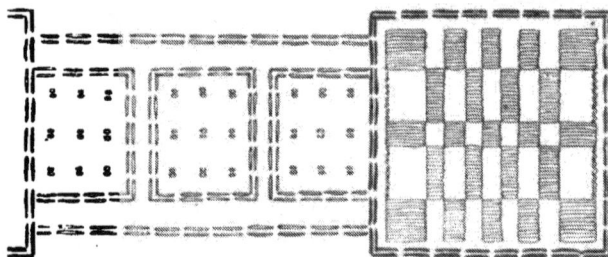

Diag. 165.

The student must above all bear in mind the method of stitchery she wishes to adopt, and plan her design that it may be well suited for this. Infinite variety may be achieved with lines and checks, and small powderings over vacant spaces, but all such lines must at first run parallel with warp and weft of the material, and it is advisable that at first the stitches

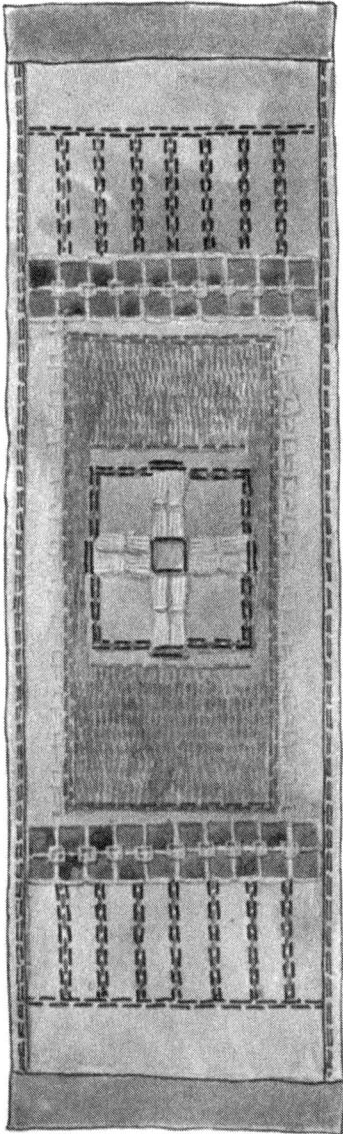 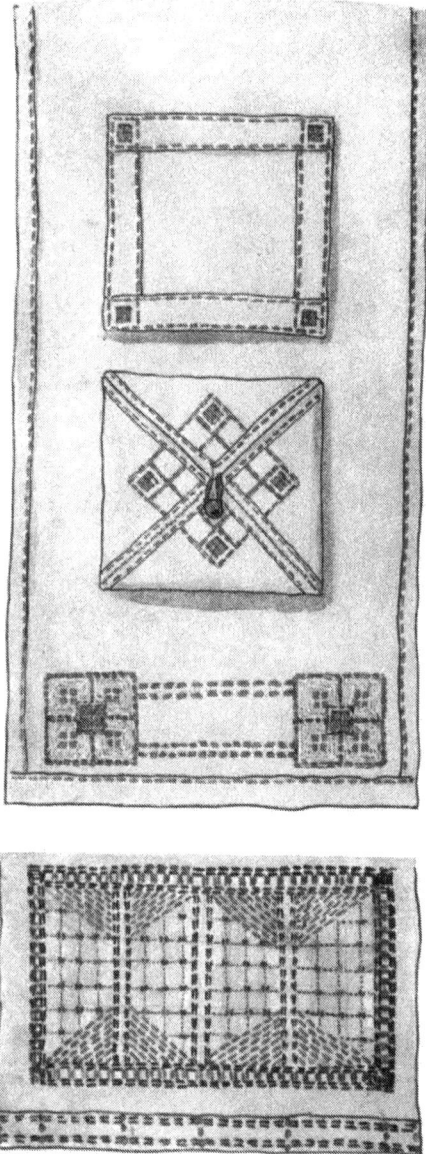

ILLUSTRATIONS OF STUDENTS' WORK. 171.

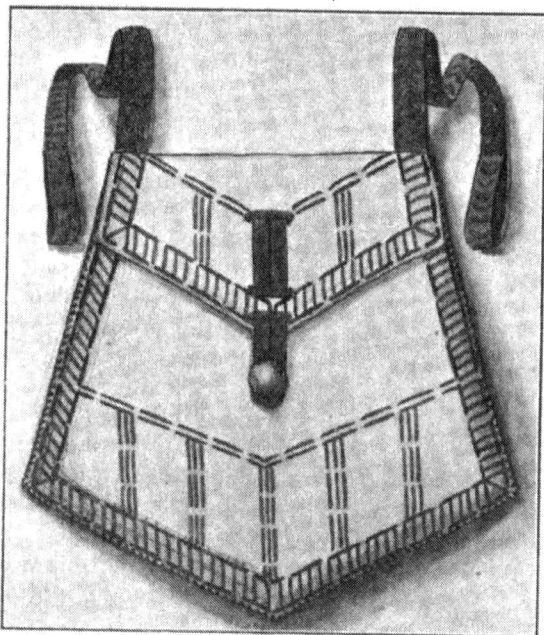

Diag. 168.

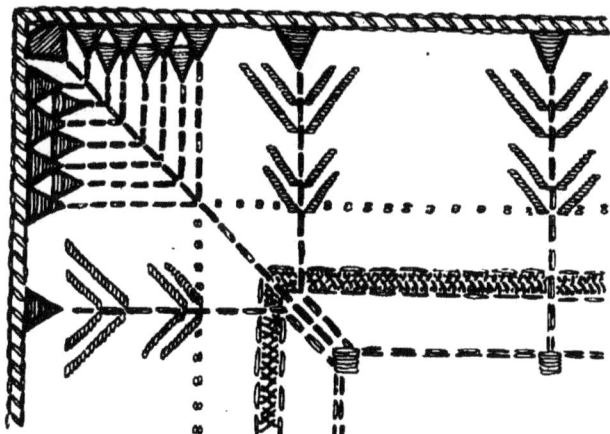

Diag. 169.

used should follow in order those learned in the earliest exercises, so that the student may learn the scope and adaptability of these stitches.

Diagrams 164–167 are carried out entirely with the "Tacking Stitch," while the hanging pocket (Diag. 168) introduces the hemming and top-sewing stitches as part of the decoration.

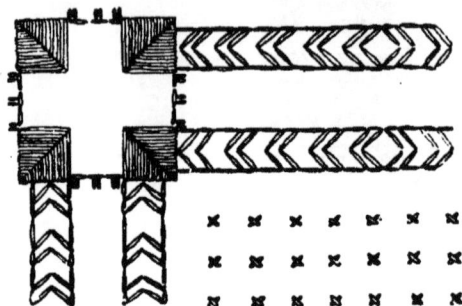

Diagrams 169, 170, and 171, show corners of a cushion, mat, and sideboard cover, and introduce diagonal lines as well as the perpendicular and horizontal ones, and here the herringbone stitch is introduced.

It cannot be too emphatically urged that the student should give herself plenty of practice in these straight-line designs, as herein lies the fundamental plan for making any good pattern on woven texture. Too many diagonal lines are not advisable, they give a restless effect, and are difficult to work on the cross of the material. The best design is that which abides by and insists upon the limitations imposed by the difficulties in working the material.

Diag. 170.

LESSON VI

MATERIAL IN RELATION TO GARMENTS AND HOUSEHOLD LINEN: REPAIR

AGE: 14–18 YEARS; 18–24 YEARS

In considering material for under and outer garments, *occupation*, *season*, and *age* decide the quality and quantity.

The baby must have soft, warm, light-weight fabric.

After the flannel binder, mixed silk and woollen woven vests are best for wearing next the skin, or simply woollen knitted vests. Diag. 172 illustrates the short bodice and skirt of a christening robe combined by means of gathering or whipping—enhanced by symbolic design suitable for the purpose of the dress.

A first shortening frock may have sleeve and bodice all in one piece (Diag. 173), and decorated by stitchery adapted to the material.

Quilting need not be merely padding inset smoothly between two pieces of material and machined down in parallel or diagonal fashion.

By means of the elementary stitchery a very beautiful bib (Diag. 174) or cot quilt (Diag. 175) may be produced. The cloak (Diag. 176) may be

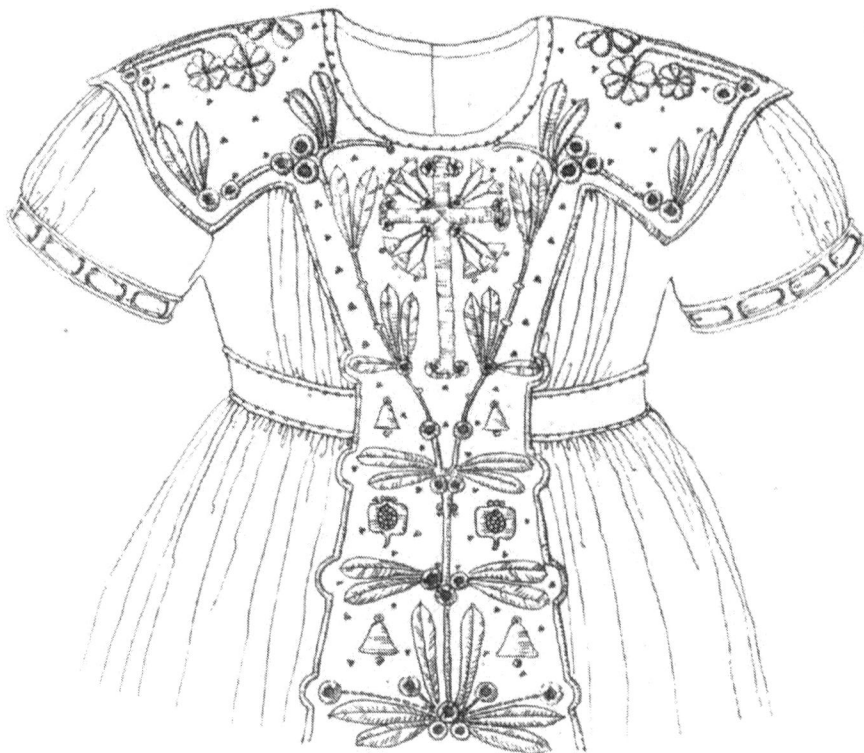

Diag. 172.

used in a modified form for the baby, or expanded into an elaborate wrap for the adult. It naturally associates itself with the infant's first jacket, and in wide material requires little shaping, except a few pleats on either shoulder. For the baby a quilted border gives weight and softness, and crossway strips, pipings, and all elementary stitching may be used advantageously as decoration.

In the strengthening of the intellectual fibre of our adolescent, *occupation* and *season* can be made an interesting factor in planning the

Diag. 173.

wardrobe. Household linen includes all articles made of cotton, woollen, linen, and damask used in our homes.

While worn cotton material may be used as dusters, two or three

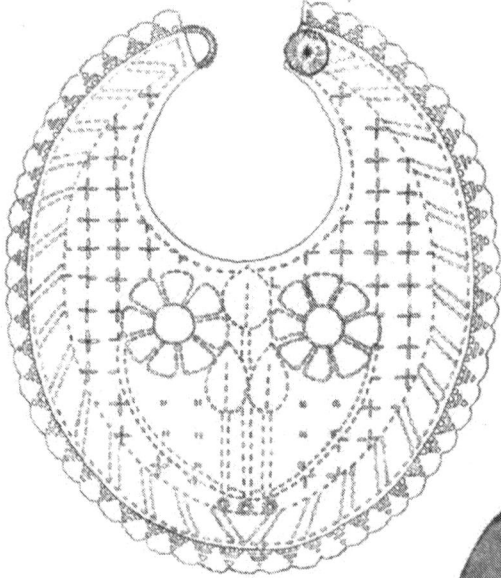

Diag. 174.

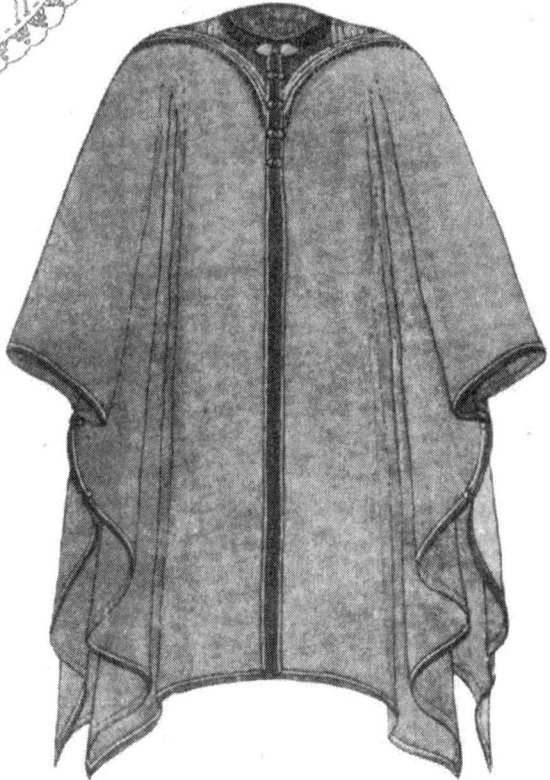

Diag. 176.

pieces joined together and used as dust sheets, worn-out blankets and flannels made into small cot blankets or under sheets, or as cloths for poultices and fomenting purposes, etc.; yet damask and linen may

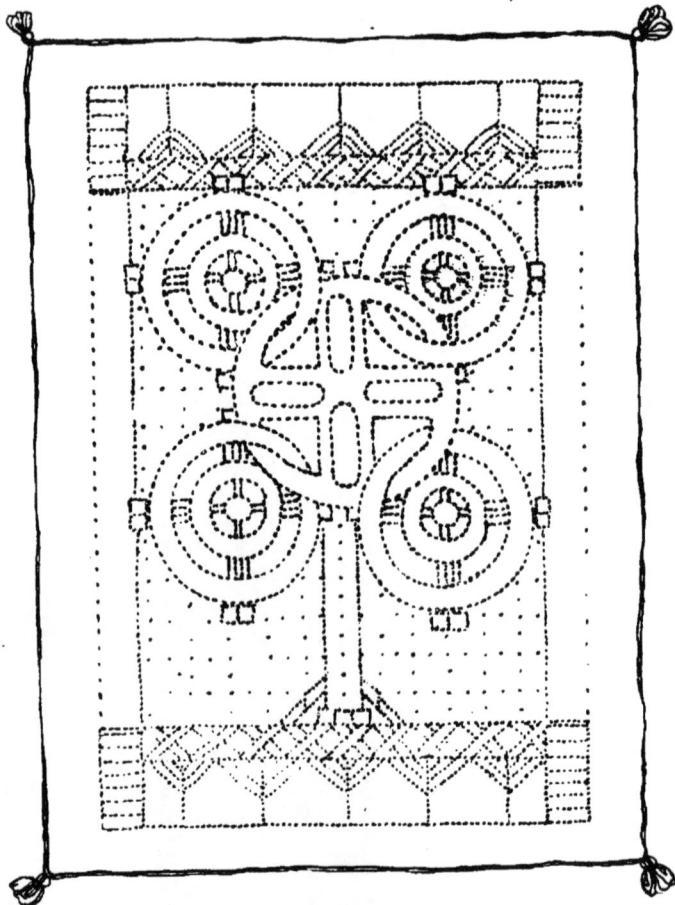

Diag. 175.

have a "knife cut" and outside garments, such as serge, may have a thorn or nail tear.

Both are mended in the same way by strands of thread crossing and recrossing, noting at the raw edges to place the needle over the

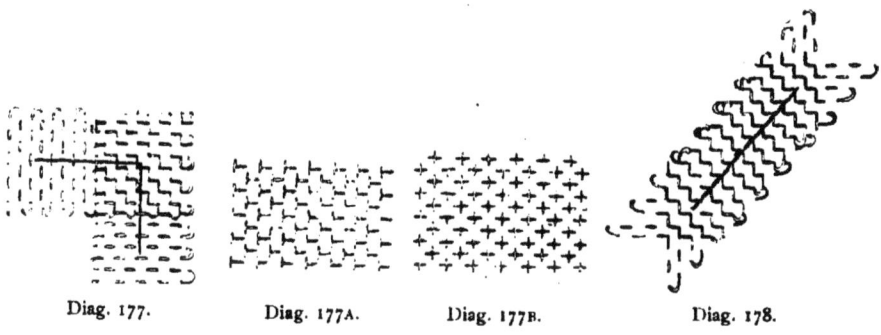

Diag. 177.

Diag. 177A.

Diag. 177B.

Diag. 178.

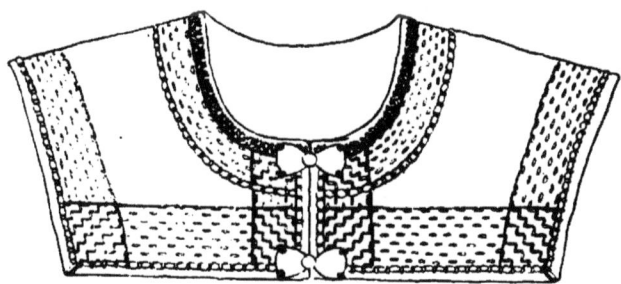

Diag. 179.

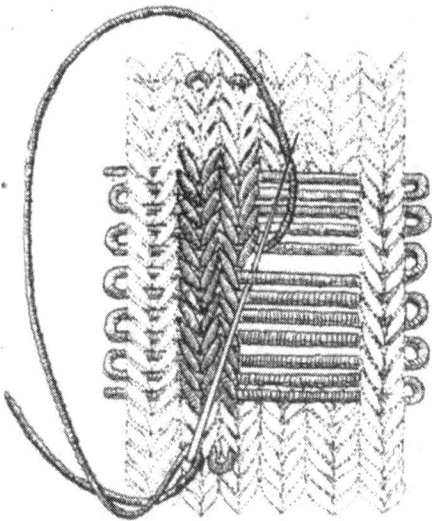

Diag. 180.

edge one way, and when coming back to place the needle underneath the edge so as to keep the edges smooth and protected (Diags. 177, 178).

As the adolescent enters the second period of skill, it is advisable to try and follow the design of the weaving with linen, silk, or woollen thread according to texture.

Diag. 179 shows the yoke of a dress decorated and strengthened by means of the hedge tear, serge or damask darn, and forms a gracious way of approaching the actual mending of the prosaic tear.

And fingers of knitted gloves, elbows of jerseys, etc., may be darned as in Diag. 180, by following the design of the knitting.

LESSON VII

DESIGNS BASED ON THE CIRCLE

AGE: 14–18 YEARS; 18–24 YEARS

OUR next stage in the making of patterns introduces the circle, and this immediately gives the designer an immensely wider field from which to gather material, since all curving lines are composed of segments of circles of varying size. But in the beginning it is advisable to keep to

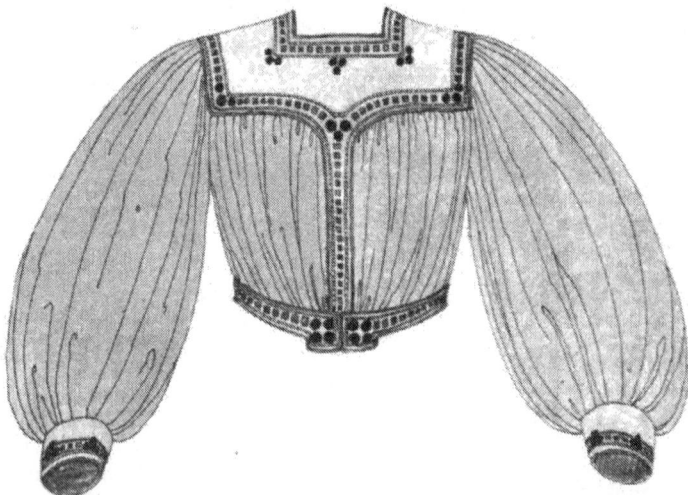

Diag. 182.

the entire sphere, without too much licence in varying it, and in order to keep steadiness and stability in the design, straight lines in some form or another are needful, though they may be merely straight lines of spots or squares. Diag. 181, a coverlet, sewn chiefly with the tacking stitch, gives an excellent example of this combination and is as simple in its construction as can be, and yet most suitable for the coarse woollen fabric on which it is worked. The worker may make use of compasses,

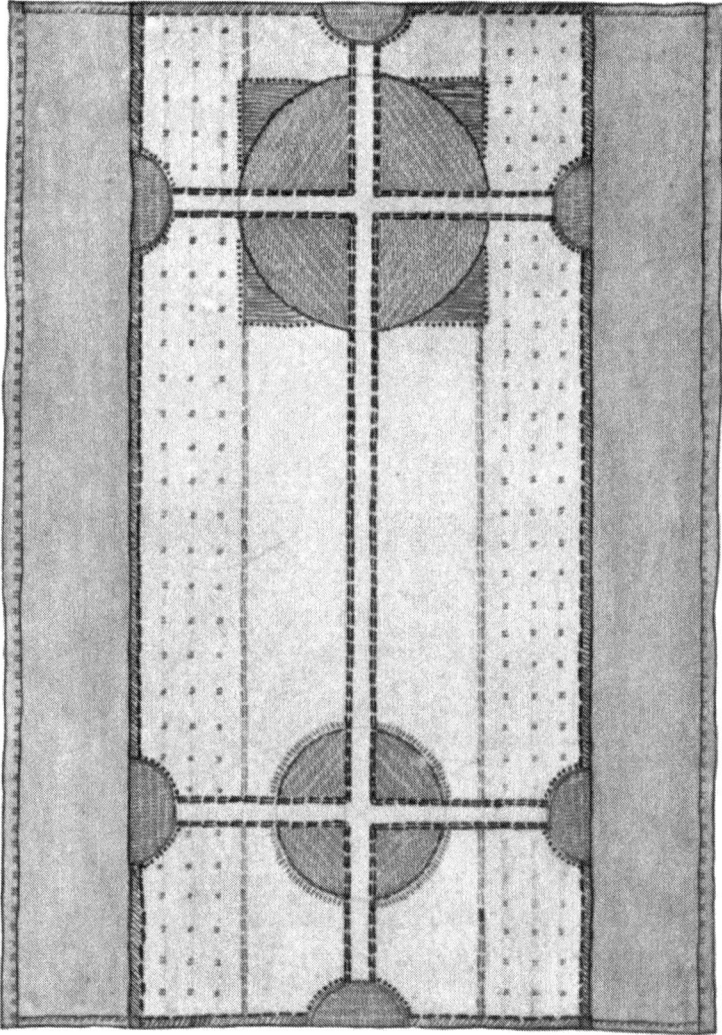

181. Coverlet of Welsh Flannel Sewn with Wool.

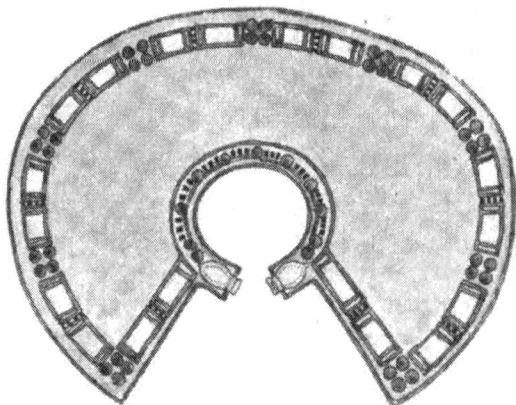

Diag. 183.

Diag. 184.

but if compasses are not at hand, a penny, a teacup, a plate, or even a round tray will prove excellent substitutes. Diags. 182, 183, 184 show a blouse and a tippet and a dress designed thus with combined straight

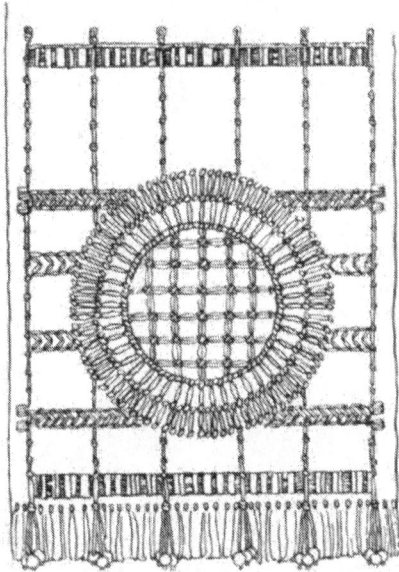

Diag. 185.

lines and circles. Diag. 185 shows the end of a toilet cloth, and the circle here has taken a floral semblance by means of its radiating straight lines of stitching.

LESSON VIII

INTRODUCTION OF THE LEAF FORM

AGE: 14–18 YEARS ; 18–24 YEARS

HERE the scope of the designer is again widened by the introduction of leaf forms—simple in outline at first, and later, if the type of leaf chosen be much complicated by serrations, it is well to design it to fit a given space of simple outlines, so that whilst keeping the individual characteristics of the leaf, it may at the same time be controlled into convenient dimensions. Diag. 186 gives some leaves of the simplest shapes, and Diag. 186A gives elaborations showing arrangements of one or more

Diag. 186.

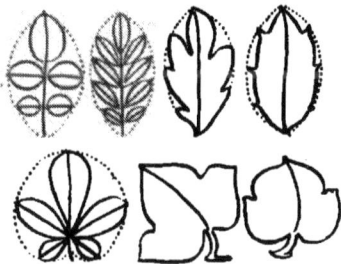

Diag. 186A.

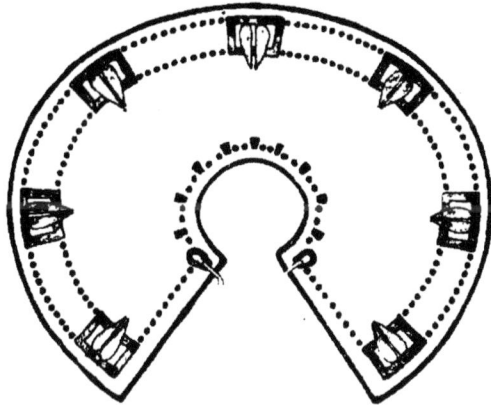

Diag. 187.

leaves to simple masses. Always draw in the main vein or " backbone " of a leaf first when designing it, thus to gain a sure way of seeing that such leaves take the right direction and grow beautifully out of their stem lines if they have any.

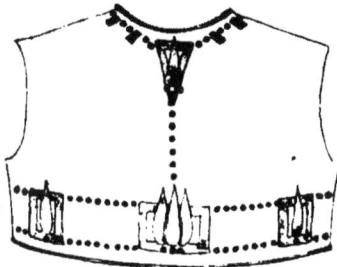

Diag. 188.

Diag. 189.

After experimenting with the leaf combined with the simple circle and the straight lines, the student can give to the circles definite floral appearance, and may now use her knowledge of botany, giving correct construction to the plants used as motives in so far as is convenient and suitable for the pattern. It is difficult to put any limit to the liberty we may take with botanical correctness. One may make use of a four-petalled flower where there ought to be five petals, but it is not desirable

Diag. 190.

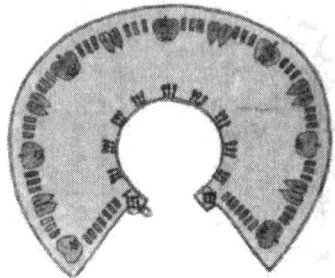

Diag. 191.

that roses should grow on ivy stems. One may turn and twist a plant which generally grows perpendicularly, but it is not good to make a cluster of such pendant flowers as laburnum to take an erect position. Such liberties must, however, be left to the choice and good taste of the designer.

Diags. 187 and 188 illustrate a child's bodice and tippet embroidered in wool with leaves and a square panel device combined with spots.

Diags. 189 and 190 illustrate the

Diag. 192.

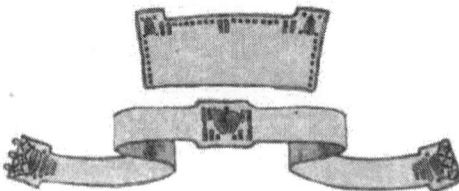

Diag. 193.

end of a sideboard or toilet cloth and a square table mat, with a design of clover.

Diags. 191, 192, a collar, belt, and cuff with a simple pattern of leaves and apples, suited for working in silk or flax on firm linen.

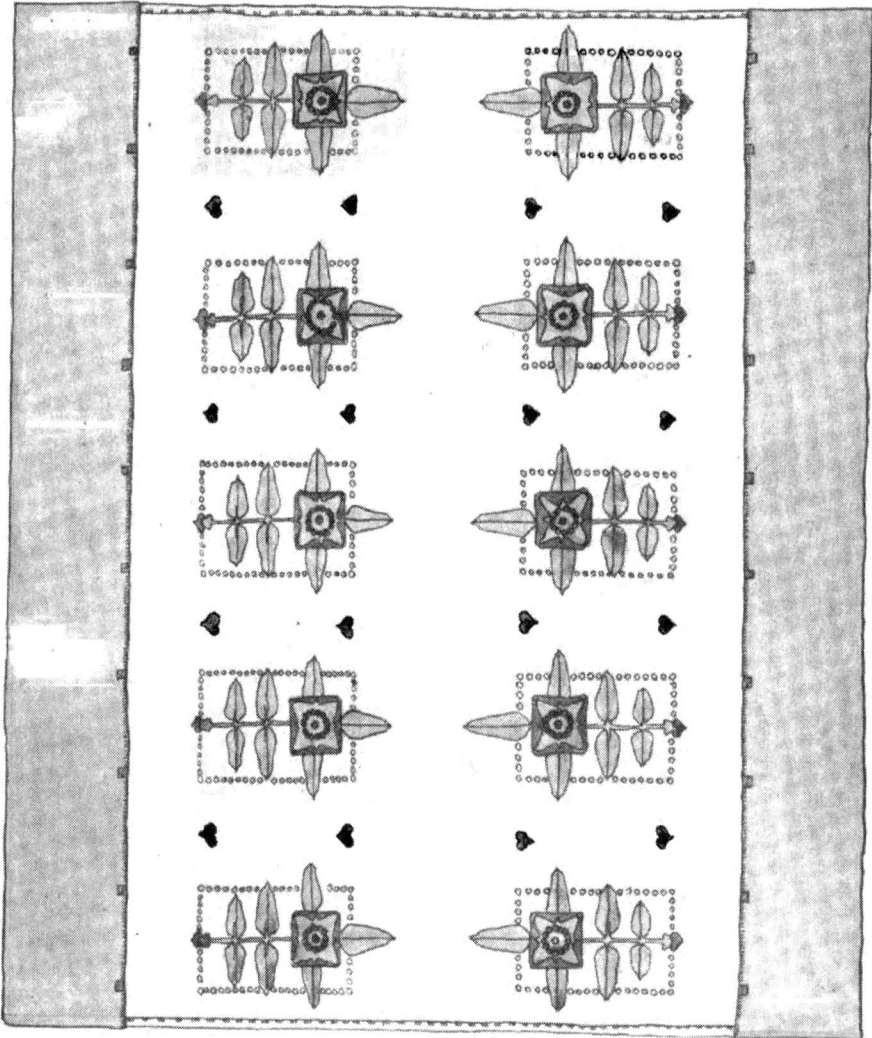

Diag. 194.

I

Diag. 193, a blouse bodice with design of square flowers, leaves and dots, suited for working in silk or cotton on woollen or linen material.

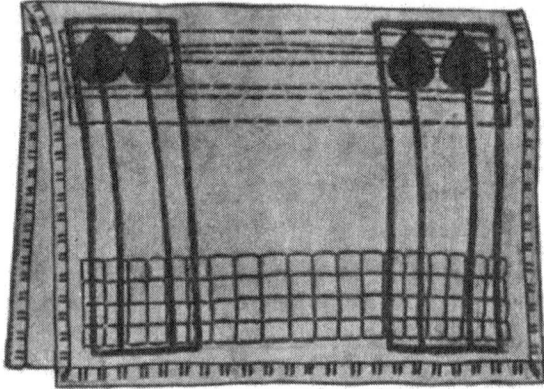

Diag. 195.

Diag. 194, a coverlet of linen with square roses and leaves contained in oblong panels.

Diag. 195, is an excellent example of a simple leaf motive combined with straight lines of darning and chain stitch.　More developed floral

Diag. 196.

forms are in Diags. 196, 197, and 198.　The first of these has the circle divided up into the more or less symmetrical petals of a rose, surrounded

197. CUSHION IN LINEN APPLIQUÉ.

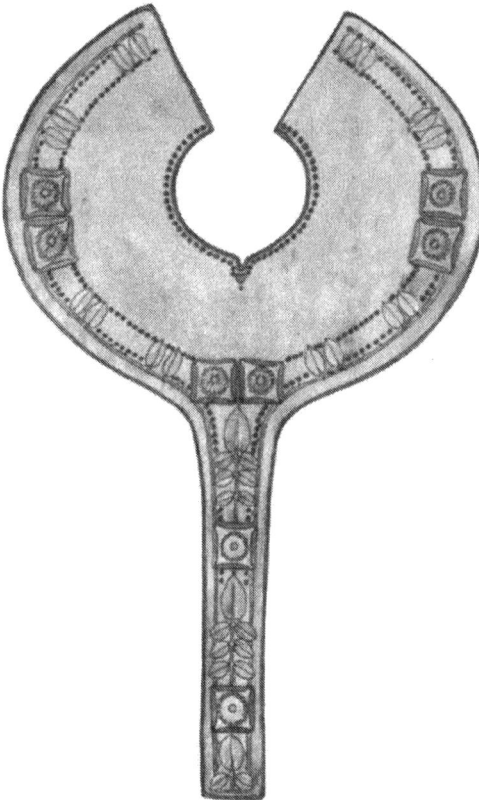

198. YOKE AND FRONT OF BLOUSE SEWN WITH SILK.

Diag. 199.

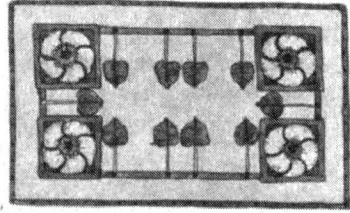

Diag. 200.

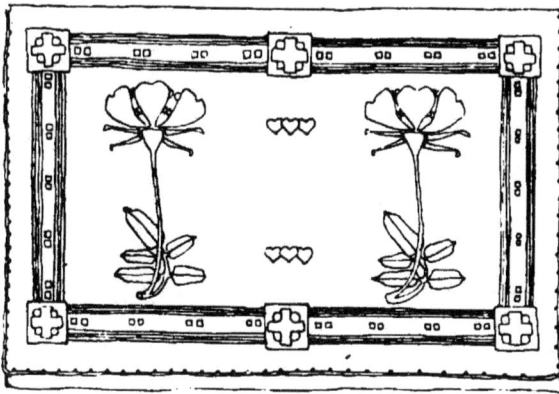

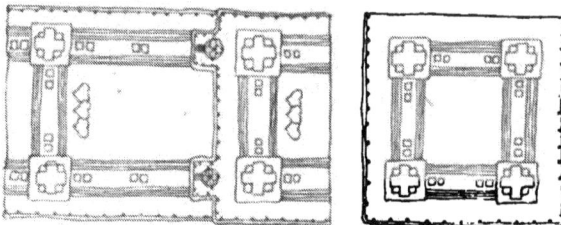

Diag. 202.

by a circle of spots. A border of heart-shaped leaves is a simple frame-work. The whole to be worked in satin stitch with silk on linen or spotted damask. Diag. 197 is a cushion with a centre panel and flowers of applied linen on linen. The circles here take another rose form more conventionalized than Diag. 196. Diag. 198 is a combined yoke and front panel for a blouse, and here the rose is again used, but in a much conventionalized square form.

Diags. 199 and 200 represent a bag and sachet on linen with a simple blossom evolved from the circle.

Diag. 201 is a portière on coarse grey linen with applied borders and

Diag. 203.

leaves of green linen and simple flowers and berries sewed in wools. The long lines of stem may be couched in coarse rug wool, one or more strands according to its thickness.

Diag. 202 illustrates nightdress, brush, and handkerchief bags of linen or silk. The floral form here is taken in profile, roughly filling a semi-circle, lines of couching connect the square-corner devices, and the whole is finished with a neat piping.

Diag. 203 gives a design of roses and leaves for a cushion, to be worked in coarse silks or wool.

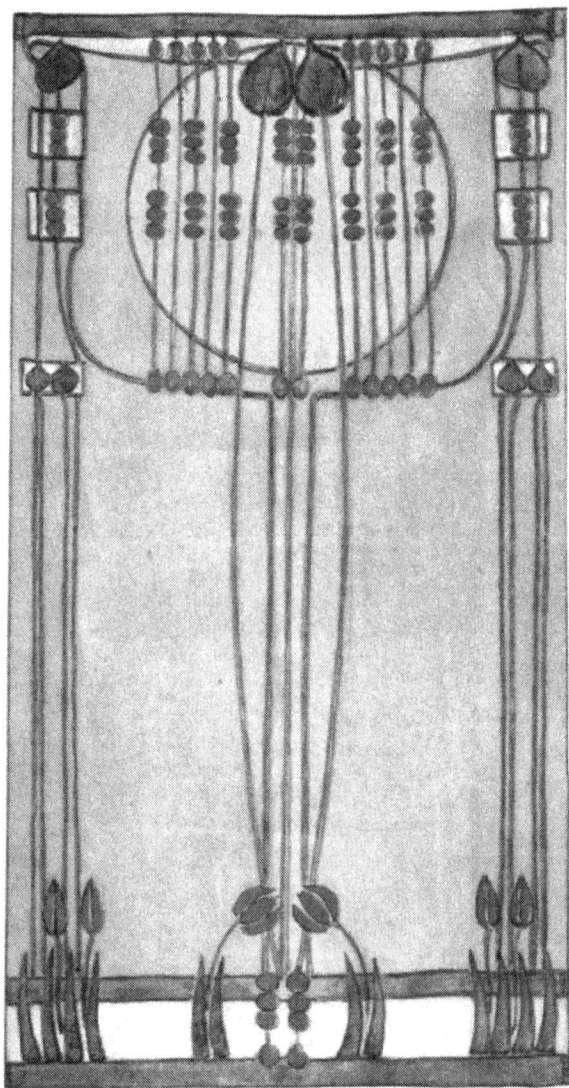

201. Curtain for a Door, Sewn with Wools.

LESSON IX

APPLIQUÉ

AGE: 14-18 YEARS; 18-24 YEARS

APPLIQUÉ work, as being an addition of applied patches of another material combined with stitchery, requires special consideration. It must, first of all, be borne in mind that the chief object in applying a patch is to save time in covering surface which would incur laborious stitching. Therefore appliqué work is only suited for designs of fairly large size, which demand broad simple effects of colour.

The choice of materials must be carefully considered, and as a general rule it is best to apply patches of the same material as the ground of the work : linen on linen, silk on silk, and woollen on woollen stuffs, so that the patch may be of the same consistency and elasticity as the background and will therefore wear better with it. Silk patches on linen or wool almost invariably fray away from the background. Velvet patches may be applied to silk or to a mixture of silk and wool, but are not suitable for other materials. *No* material can be applied in patches to a velvet ground with success.

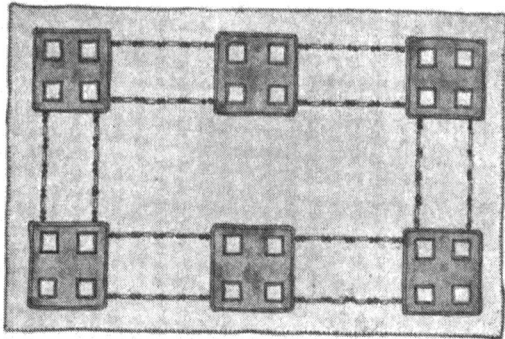

Diag. 204.

Diag. 205.

Linen is distinctly the best material for appliqué work, and washes and wears excellently.

The method of working it is as follows.

Carefully trace the shape of the applied patches with the warp and weft corresponding to that of the background they are to cover. Cut these out and tack or overcast them firmly into place. It is even permissible to paste these on if the work will not require to be washed. The best stitch to use round these patches is a close satin stitch about $\frac{1}{4}$ inch wide. Button-hole stitch may also be used, or two rows of couching

Diag. 206.

Diag. 207.

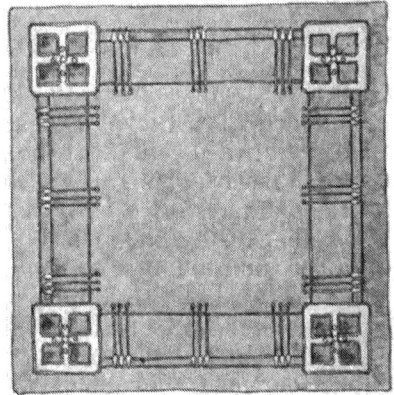

Diag. 208.

Diag. 209.

with a thick thread. This outline of stitching must always be akin in colour and tone to the applied patch, so that it will be distinct from the colour of the background.

Always set the needle into the patch and bring it out at the edge when stitching it on, or there will be a tendency to give the patch a blistered appearance.

If the tacking threads are close enough to the edge of the material they will be covered by the stitching and need not be withdrawn.

The shapes used for applied patches must as far as

possible be simple in outline, without any superfluous serrations or
narrow bands. Stems, except in very large designs, can be better and
more quickly executed by stitchery alone.

Diag. 210.

Diag. 204 is an excellent example of straight line in appliqué; the
square patches have square holes cut out of them, and all the raw edges
are covered with satin stitch.

Diag. 211.

Diag. 212.

Diag. 205 is another square patch with a round hole.

Diags. 206 and 207 square patches again, connected with lines of
spots in satin stitch or with straight lines of couching.

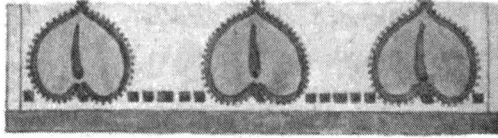

Diag. 213.

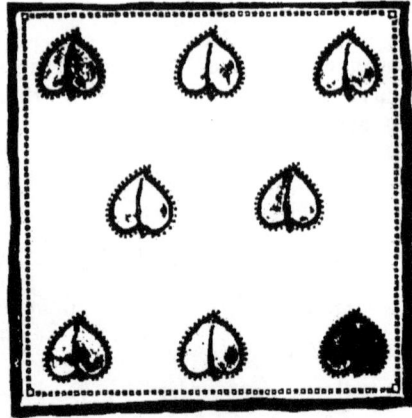

Diag. 214.

Diag. 215.

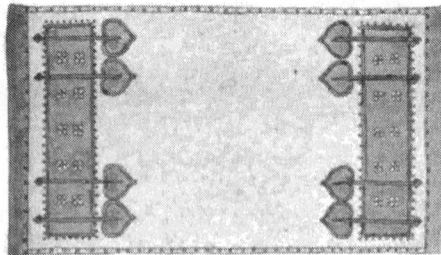

Diag. 216.

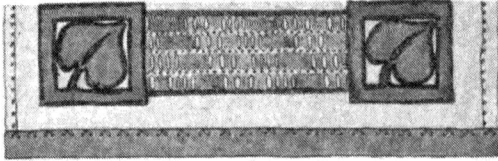

Diag. 217.

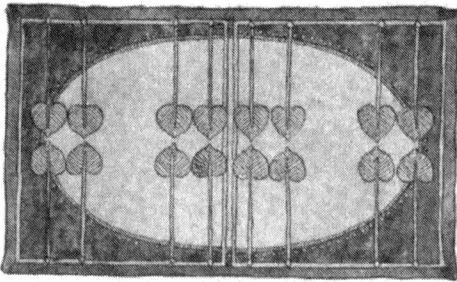

Diag. 218.

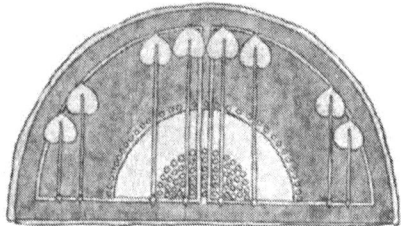

Diag. 219.

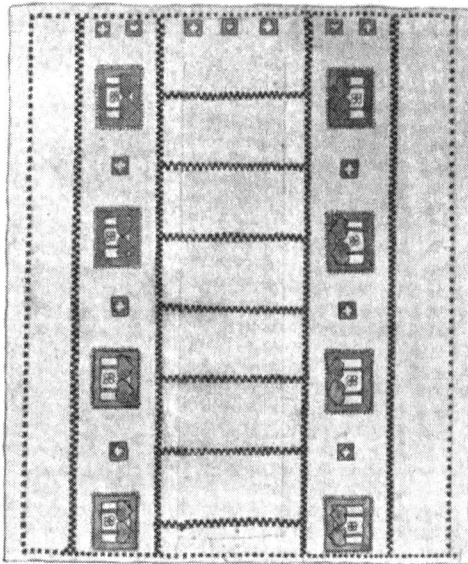

Diag. 220.

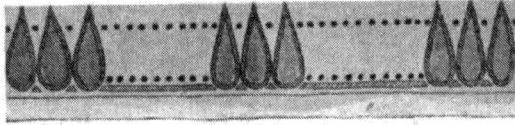

Diag. 221.

Diag. 222.

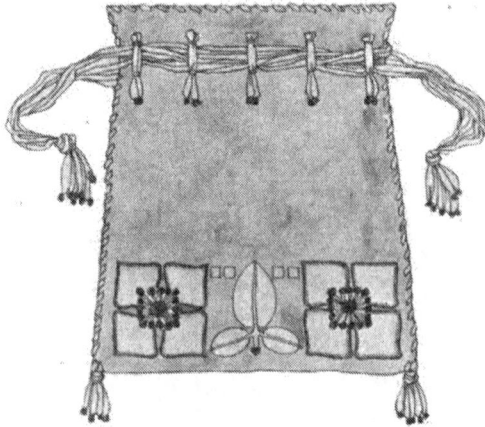

Diag. 223.

Diag. 224.

Diags. 208 and 209 give a simple square leaf-shaped patch with connecting lines of stem or spots.

Diags. 210, 211, 212 give various applications of the heart shape;

Diag. 225.

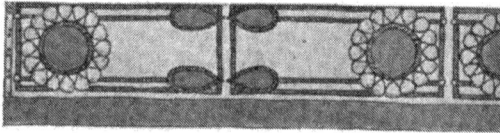

Diag. 226.

and 213, 214, 215, 216, 217, 218, 219 are all different applications of the heart-shaped leaf form, combined with borders of spots or open drawn work. Diag. 220 is a suggestion for a coverlet which might be made of three strips of roller towelling, the selvedges joined by means of satin stitch in small chequers. Diag. 221 is another leaf form arranged in a very simple pattern for a border of a curtain.

Diag. 222 is a combination of the latter with a four-petalled flower. Diags. 223 and 224 show square flowers of clematis combined with a leaf form; while 225 shows the circle modified into an apple shape, combined with leaves and hem stitching.

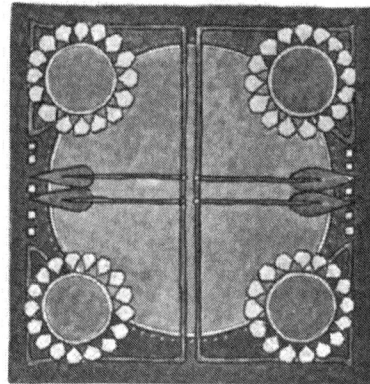

Diag. 227.

Diags. 226 and 227 are circular and leaf-shaped patches forming daisies, for a border and cushion.

LESSON X

VARIOUS materials demand various methods of marking pattern, but for the average household goods of fairly light colours, the quickest and most direct method is to make a clear tracing of the pattern on firm tracing paper, or, if many repeats are needed, on linen tracing sheet.

This must then be carefully set in place on the material on a drawing board and two drawing pins inserted at one side ; now slip in a sheet of red, blue, or (if the material be dark) black carbon paper, and pin down the traced sheet again at the other sides, taking care not to set the pins through the carbon sheet. Trace through this with a hard short pencil or a stylus, keeping the pencil at such a low angle that it may be drawn after the hand (if it be kept upright it cuts the paper).

Be very careful that no buttons or bracelets are worn on the wrist while tracing, or they will make untidy marks on the material.

Dark materials are best to be marked as follows. Draw the pattern out on firm cartridge paper, and prick the lines with a very stout darning needle on some padded surface, making about four holes to the inch. Pin this on the material on a board, and take a small sponge dipped into Chinese white paint (water colour in tubes is the best). Squeeze the paint out on a small dish and use it as dry as possible, and pounce it through the holes on to the material. This method is good for marking thick woollens, arras cloths, and other surfaces which will not take impression from carbon paper.

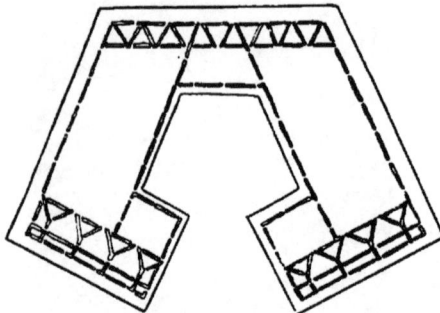

Diag. 228.

Another excellent method for marking woolly or pile surfaces, like velvet, is to cut a simple stencil in oiled sheet, such as is used in a copying press, and this may be stencilled through with the Chinese white paint, which must be used very dry, so that no drops collect underneath the paper. Diag. 228 shows such a stencil cut, and 229 shows the same worked out fully on velvet. It will be noted that the smaller details need not be cut in the stencil, they can quite easily be marked in with a slight line of tacking if they cannot be sewn direct without marking. In such a stencil only half the design need be cut, and when one half is marked the paint may be washed away and the stencil turned over and the whole pattern completed.

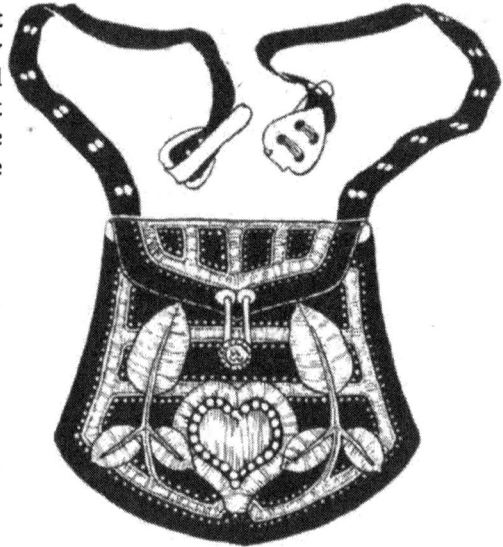

Diag. 229.   Diag. 230.

Diag. 230 illustrates a velvet pocket marked off in this way and sewn in satin stitch with beads and French knots. Such a bag would require a stiff canvas or leather lining pasted on before it is made up.

Thin transparent materials may be pinned tightly *over* the drawing and it may be traced through with a pencil.

LESSON XI

COLOUR AND TONE

AGE: 14–18 YEARS; 18–24 YEARS

THERE are no rules to be given as to colour schemes which may not be broken with legitimacy. All depends on the proportion in which contrasting lines or masses are arranged, and the quantity of space these occupy.

And here it is well to make clear a too frequently mistaken use of terms, namely, the confusion between the words "tone" and "colour." These are not in any sense synonymous. "Colour" is the general term for the varying pigment or dye, or the spectroscopic quality of light; and "tone" is applied to the quantity, the lightness or depth of the colour. "Colour" may be said to be equivalent to "Key" in music, while "tone" has also its corresponding meaning in the technical phraseology of the kindred art.

If we are planning the colour scheme of a piece of work, it is well at the outset to consider first the colour of the material with regard to that of the place where it is to be used, if we know of this definitely. Then we must make up our minds as to what colour we would wish to preponderate in the scheme, and whether the tone of the pattern is as a whole to be light or dark against the background.

A very excellent plan is then to fix on some combining "atmosphere" of colour with which all the larger masses of the pattern may be blended. We take the three primary colours, Red, Blue, and Yellow. Say that we take red for our combining colour, then all the blues we use must be tinted slightly with red, which makes them purplish; and all yellows will become somewhat orange with the admixture of the red, any greens used should tend to be rather grey with this added colour.

In like manner if we take the blue as an "atmosphere," then reds must be purple, and yellows must be greenish. This arrangement need not apply to very small points of colour, but it is a fairly safe plan to guide the beginner to good harmonizing of the main masses of ornament. Greys, which are combined of all three primary colours, may partake of any one or two in greater proportion than another, and thus greys may be reddish, yellow, blue, greenish or purplish, and the choice in such intricacies of colour combination must depend on their general relation to the other colours employed.

On white or very light grounds the colours used should be clear and bright, and save in slight and somewhat linear patterns, they should not be too deep in tone.

A ground of medium tone, neither very dark nor very light, may be decorated with a pattern which includes both lighter and darker tones; .but it is well that the main masses of such pattern be kept either entirely lighter or entirely darker than the groundwork, and only small points of detail should differ from the general tone of the whole.

It is rarely wise to make a design which has an equal quantity of extremely light and extremely dark colour evenly disposed over its whole surface. This tends to give the painfully dazzling effect shown in some of the now somewhat out-of-date foulard silks which were used for ladies' dresses, and which were far from pleasing to look at. "All over" designs are best carried out in tones which do not greatly contrast from their background.

In planning coloured designs it is well to bear in mind that the variety of stitches employed should not be too great. Embroidery does *not* exist to show off our knowledge of stitches. It is in all-white or monochrome designs that the play of varying stitches is needful, just as we require greater variety of texture in modelled or sculptured surfaces, as opposed to the even, smooth surface of a painting.

As a general rule, a certain reticence is desirable in the use of the more assertive colours, such as hot browns, terra cottas, scarlet or orange. These do not readily fall into scheme with the general colouring of the average room, if they are used in large quantities. A fairly safe range of colours may be found if we confine ourselves to those generally seen in the landscapes we look at, where (like mercy mixed in everything) blue preponderates, in the greens, greys, and purples of its foreground and distance.

LESSON XII

FIGURE DESIGN FOR EMBROIDERY.

THE treatment of the human figure in embroidery has always been the highest and most difficult achievement of the craft, and the methods of working employed are a somewhat vexed question. First and foremost, the designer must be a good draughtsman, able to treat the figure and its draperies in such a way as to lend them most easily to execution in silken or woollen thread and texture. Any slavish copying of a painting is undesirable; needlework does not make good paint, nor is it needful to torture one material into ineffectual imitation of another. If the effect of painting is desired, paint is the medium which most quickly arrives at that effect. Embroidery has characteristics so exclusively and beautifully its own that it should be the aim of its designer to make use of these to their fullest extent, without straining the material beyond the limits to which its texture confines it.

Therefore it is not needful to treat flesh tints in difficult and intricate shading of tone. Better it is to treat the face, for instance, by means of simple and dignified outlines in suitable neutral tint, while if the figure be on a small scale the folds of garments can be worked simply as masses of colour formed by satin stitching carefully and regularly between the lines of drawing. This demands that the width of each fold must be designed so that it is not too wide to be crossed by a single stitch. Shading of colour in this method is very successfully managed by gradually working one tone or tint into another. Such embroidered drapery has a very rich effect. If the work be on large scale it may consist of masses of darning defined by outlines, or by applied material with the drapery lines defined by couching of silk or braid, and added ornament of borders or powdered pattern may be shown in enrichments of stitchery.

The treatment of hair is good if drawn in separate locks, sewn across with satin stitch, always taking the stitch directly across the lock, as in embroidering folds. The curving of the folds gives wonderful play of light to the glossy silks.

Another more tedious but very beautiful method of making hair in large figures is to couch it in single threads of gold tinsel or silk.

For small figure panels no material lends itself so kindly as good satin of some pale colour. It is so firm and smooth, the intricacies of the drawing may be so accurately marked and so easily followed by the stitchery. Such material can with ease be worked on the hand, but for larger panels, where elaborate couching is needful on applied material, it is best to paste the appliqué into place and sew on a large frame till all outlines are complete. Masses of gold stitchery, couching, or the radiations of a nimbus, are best done on tight material on the frame, while enrichments of satin stitch, etc., may be more expeditiously executed on the hand. In fact, for almost all ordinary work a frame is quite unnecessary if the material be firm (Frontispiece and Diag. 231).

LESSON XIII

FINISHINGS

FITNESS of finish is the crowning completion of needlecraft, and often it is in the so-termed "finishings," the dainty conceits of construction, that the whole charm of a beautiful piece of work lies.

Hems and seams in themselves can produce beautiful results without further addition of ornament. Piping, bindings, and borders of colours

TRAVELLERS' JOY.
A PANEL ON SATIN BY ANN MACBETH.
DIAGRAM 231.

differing from the fabric of the work make good decoration in themselves, and ingenious tricks of making latchets, ties, and fastenings often give distinction to work that without it would lack interest. All manner of unexpected material can be used to give a decorative effect; braid, corset cord, carpet binding, even twine, if of suitable colour, may be used to give completeness of finish to our garments and other embroidered possessions. Wool of all thicknesses may be applied, from the thick rug wool to finest mending wools—as fringes—or to give a strong outline

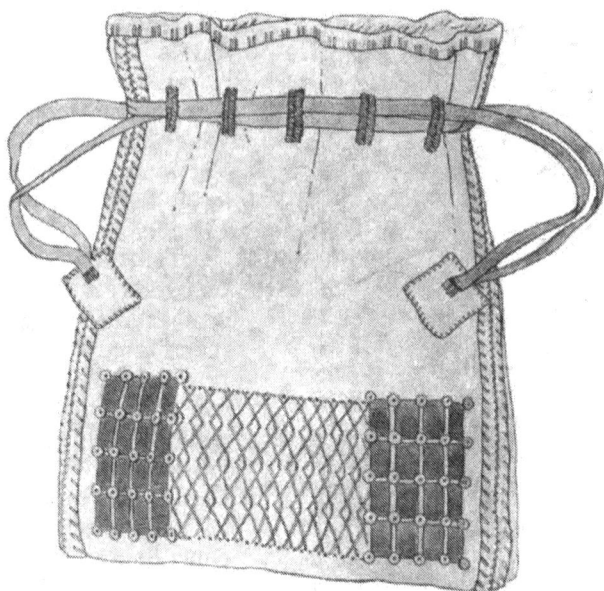

Diag. 232.

where the pattern is of a scale to demand it. Beads also of all sorts may be used to give richness and weight to such materials as are suited for them; but it is well to remember that, if work is to be washed, beads may be inconveniently in the way of successful laundering; they are, on the whole, most suited to the decoration of velvet or heavy materials which do not require to be cleaned. Beads may be used in fringes, or if they be flat, they may be sewed on to the material. As a general rule, it is best to use those which have rounded surfaces, not cut into facets, as the latter have a less rich effect and are too assertively sparkling. Ties

K

and cords may be completed with rich tassels of silk, wool or leather, or may be enclosed in little embroidered tags (Diag. 232), or finished with beads. Cords may be made of silk, wool, or linen, and drawstrings and ties may be made of single or manifold strands of ribbon, pleated or knotted, in all manner of ways.

Pipings may be set into place by means of dainty French knots, or by a whipping of coloured thread; latchets and button-loops may be made beautiful by being made of cord or thin braid, the ends laid along the material for some distance and then coiled into large spirals.

Buttons may be used in a purely ornamental way, or if they are large may be themselves decorated to fit the style of the article they fasten (Diag. 233).

The cleverest devisers of "fashions" are those ingenious men and women who invent such fitments as these to the garments they design— without using much added trimming. We still admire such things, even as they were admired by those who wrote of the construction of the curtains and hangings of the Tabernacle, of the hems and borders and the bindings of

Diag. 233.

those glorious garments of the high priest; and "wise-hearted" is the word applied to those who made them. Wise-hearted also let us be, and the wisdom may come in the doing of these things, and we may leave behind us a fairer heritage for our daughters, for in the works of our hands they shall know us when we ourselves have gone.

MATERIALS, AND WHERE TO GET THEM

It has been thought advisable to give the particulars of various materials suitable for the work suggested in the foregoing chapters, with names of the manufacturers, for the convenience of readers.

Calico in white and unbleach, and coloured casement cottons, may be had in excellent quality almost anywhere, and there is no need to specify any maker; but for cotton materials and linens in colour, the most durable are to be had from the various agents of Messrs. Alexander Morton & Co., whose many and beautiful Sundour Fabrics are absolutely fast to both sunlight and washing. These range in price from 1s. per yard upwards, and are excellent for household use and for dresses.

The agent for these fabrics in Canada is: G. Kitchen, c/o A. Morton & Co., Empire Buildings, Wellington St., Toronto; and in New York: Messrs. Witcombe-McGeachin & Co., 874, Broadway.

A great choice of flannels at low prices may be had from Messrs. Pryce Jones, Ltd., Newtown, North Wales, and Calgary, Canada.

Linen sheetings and roller towelling of all kinds, and also coloured linens, may be got at very low prices and in most excellent quality from Messrs. Murphy and Orr, Donegall Street, Belfast.

We take this opportunity to mention the only variety of flannelette which is not highly inflammable. The fatalities due to the use of flannelette as usually sold are very numerous, and there is considerable underestimation on the part of the public as to its danger. Flannelette will not ignite if laid flat on the table, but if the flame catches it in a vertical position it runs up it with great rapidity and is most dangerous. W. H. Perkin, Ph.D., F.R.S., Professor of Chemistry to the University of Manchester, has produced an *absolutely non-inflammable* variety, known as NONFLAM, which may be had from drapers, or at 3, Piccadilly, Manchester, at about one penny per yard more than the ordinary flannelettes.

A very good cotton fabric, known as Celtic Canvas, which is very suitable for curtains, coverlets, and dresses, is to be had in unbleach and colours from Messrs. Brown and Beveridge, Sauchiehall Street, Glasgow;

it is very wide—72 to 100 inches—and costs from 1s 6d. upwards. This firm also supplies a beautiful thick, dull-finished embroidery silk, known as Tyrián, in beautiful colouring—especially suited for work on velvet or for large bold designs. They are also agents for Sundour Fabrics.

Coloured embroidery cotton may be had in a large range of colours from any agent for Messrs. Clark & Co., Paisley; it is made in various thicknesses and is known as "Coton à Broder," and is specially recommended for the work in the elementary scheme in this book.

A very excellent range of woollen yarns, suitable for the elementary needlecraft scheme and for knitting, is to be had from Messrs. J. & J. Baldwin, Halifax, England. These may be had in both hanks and in penny balls, under the name of White Heather Scotch Fingering. The balls are of a thickness suitable for mending and for embroidery.

A very fine range of colours in rug wools may be had from this firm, which are excellent also for large bold embroidery work.

Embroidery silks of all kinds may be had from Messrs. Jas. Pearsall & Sons, Little Britain, London, and are easily got at their agencies anywhere. Mallard, Cable, and Filo Floss silks are specially recommended for embroidery work, and may be had in a very large range of colours.

Scientific needles may be had from Messrs. Kirkby Beard & Co., Redditch. Small and large darners and crewel needles may be had from any needle manufacturers.

Teachers and those who are far from large towns would find it of immense assistance to have shade cards from these makers from which to choose and order materials.

SUGGESTED SCHEME OF WORK FOR AN ELEMENTARY SCHOOL

Division	Age	Stitchery	Construction	Material	Cost.
Infants	6–7 years	I. Tacking	Tray cloth or small mat	Coloured embroidery thread, No. 16; Unbleached calico, 12" × 9", or 12" × 12"; Needles, No. 2, sharps (Scientific)	1d.
Junior II.	7–7½ years	I. Top-sewing	Small bag; Handkerchief case; Making of cords	Coloured embroidery thread, No. 16; Unbleached calico, 12" × 9", or 12" × 12"; Needles, No. 2, sharps (Scientific)	1½d.
"	7½–8 "	II. Large Hemming, *i.e.* tacking in slanting direction; III. Tacking	Lap-bag	Coloured embroidery thread, No. 16; Unbleached calico, 12" × 9", or 12" × 12"; Needles, No. 2, sharps (Scientific)	1½d.
				Unbleached calico, 36" wide, 36" × 18" (two out of 1 yard)	4½d.
Junior I.	8–9 years	I. Sew and fell (large combination)	Cushion slip or night-dress bag	Coloured embroidery thread, No.18; Unbleached calico, 36" × 12" (36" wide); Coloured calico, 36" × 6" (30"–31" wide) (two pieces)	5d.
		II. Tacking has become smaller, *i.e.* running	Sash curtains	No. 3 sharps (Scientific needles); Unbleached calico, 1 yard; Coloured calico, ½ yard	6½d.–8d.
Senior III.	9–10 years	I. Pleating	I. Overall or cooking apron	I. Unbleached calico, 1½–2 yards; Coloured calico, ½ yard; Coloured embroidery thread, No. 20; No. 5, sharps (Scientific)	1s. 1d.
		II. Herring-boning; Single darning, *i.e.* finer tacking; Sewing on of tapes; Pinking	II. Needlecase	II. Flannel; Coloured embroidery thread, No. 20; No. 5, sharps (Scientific), or fine mending yarn with small darning needles; Linen and tape, ribbon or braid	2½d.

Division	Age	Stitchery	Construction	Material	Cost.
Senior II.	10–11 years	I. Flannel seams	I. Infants' first jacket. Turn-over collars	I. Flannel—cream or coloured (two out of ¼ yard) Embroidery thread, No. 30, or mending yarn. Needles, No. 5, sharps (Scientific), or small darning needle	5½d.
		II. Button-holing (known as blanket and embroidery stitch)	II. Bookmarkers	II. III. Linen—embroidery Thread, No. 30, needles, No. 5, sharps	1½d.
		III. Chain-stitching; stitching (merely a vertical button-hole stitch)	III. Mats, etc.		
		IV. Flannel binding	IV. Kettle-holder or child's vest	IV. Flannel, any colour. Tape, braid, or ribbon	2d. 5d.
		V. Single darning (fine tacking)			
Senior I.	11–12 years (qualifying class)	I. Darning (weaving)	I. Runners, mats, book-covers, bags	I. Linen, serge, any kind of woven material. Ordinary worsted thread	2d.–3d.
		II. Strengthening strip	II. Pocket or overall pinafore, such as djibbah	II. Flannel, cotton, or linen. Tapes, braids, or a strip of another material	2d.–4d.
		III. Run and fell. Counter hem. Buttons and button-holes. Tucking, gathering, stroking, and setting in	III. Slip bodice. tucker or collar	III. *White* calico, 1 yard; No. 6, *between* (Scientific); four-six buttons. No. 40 thread, white embroidery thread	8d.–10d.
Supplementary	12–13 years	I. Eyelet-holes	I. Blouse (from the slip bodice pattern of the Qualifying Stage) with type for sleeve and yoke	I. Print, fine serge or unbleached calico, etc. (2½–3 yards, depending on width of material). Needles, No. 36 or 40 thread	1s. 3d.–3s. 6d.
			or		
		II. Sewing on hooks and eyes	II. Nightdress (from the slip bodice pattern with expanded sleeve)	II. A. White calico, or unbleached nun's veiling (bleached flour bags at 3d. each; four make a nightdress). B. Union (wool and cotton mixed). C. Flannelette (Dr. Perkin's non-flam., 4½–6 yards)	1s.–5s.

Division.	Age.	Stitchery.	Construction.	Material.	Cost.
		III. Gussets (double, single)	III. Overall (from the slip bodice pattern with modified sleeve), or	III. Any of the standard cotton materials (2½–3½ yards)	2s.–3s.
		IV. Patching, mending, darning	IV. Child's coat with sleeve from type.	IV. Unbleached calico, holland and coloured linen; button moulds, mending yarn; ordinary sewing cotton, No. 6, between (1½–2 yards)	1s. 6d.–2s.
		V. Machining	V. Baby's caps, dust caps, aprons, casement curtains (all to illustrate the various kinds of patching)	V. Any oddments of material	
Supplementary	13–14 years	I. Piping	I. Type for petticoat or skirt (housemaid's dress with slip bodice type above), or pinafore dress (skirt and bodice like djibbah or chemise)	I. White calico or any of the standard coloured materials. Print, lustre, flannel (2½–5 yards)	1s. 6d.–5s. 6d.
		II. Marking	II. Type for drawers	Any of the standard cotton or flannel materials	6d.–2s. 6d.
			1. Baby's pilch—all seat, no legs	1. ½ yard	
			2. Girl of 6 years—¾ seat, ¾ width at knee	2. 1 yard	
			3. Girl of 14 years—⅔ seat, ⅔ width at knee	3. 1½–1¾ yards	
			4. Woman's size—½ seat, ⅔ width at knee	4. 1¾–2½ yards	
		III. Darning in different kinds of material			
		IV. Machining			

KNITTING SCHEMES

Age.	Stitch.	Application.
6–7 years	Garter stitch	Kettle holder, slippers or scarf
7–8 ,,	Plain and purl	Semmit—one-third ribbed, body plain
8–9 ,,	Plain and purl—casting on and off with two needles	Pair of cuffs
9–10 ,,	Casting on and off with three needles, as for stocking-intakes	Bachelor cosy, pair of sleeves or jersey
10–11 ,,	Setting heel of stocking, turning and taking in	Pair of child's socks
11–12 ,,	All previous stitches, with addition of intakes of toe and finishing off	Stocking or sock
12–14 ,,	Re-footing, and *knitting* small edgings for the finishing of underwear or household linen	

CUTTING-OUT SCHEME

Age.	Cutting out.
6–7 years	Neckband (in paper)
7–8 ,,	Neckband, wristband (in paper)
8–9 ,,	Neckband, wristband, waistband (in paper)
9–10 ,,	Neck, wrist, waist, armhole (in paper)
10–11 ,,	Neck, wrist, waist, armhole, bust (in paper)
11–12 ,,	Neck, wrist, waist, armhole, bust, length back and front (slip-bodice type) and chemise (in cheap unbleached calico or scrim)
12–14 ,,	1. Sleeve type (with slip bodice type given) expands into nightdress, overall, blouse, child's coat
	2. Petticoat type expands into skirts (wrapper or morning dress), simple cotton dresses
	3. Drawers (types): 1. Baby's pilch—all seat, no leg
	2. Girl of 6 years—¾ seat, ¾ width at knee
	3. Girl of 14 years—⅝ seat, ¾ width at knee
	4. Woman's size—½ seat—⅝ width at knee

PRINTED BY WILLIAM CLOWES AND SONS, LIMITED, LONDON AND BECCLES.

RETURN TO the circulation desk of any
University of California Library
or to the
NORTHERN REGIONAL LIBRARY FACILITY
Bldg. 400, Richmond Field Station
University of California
Richmond, CA 94804-4698

ALL BOOKS MAY BE RECALLED AFTER 7 DAYS
- 2-month loans may be renewed by calling
  (510) 642-6753
- 1-year loans may be recharged by bringing
  books to NRLF
- Renewals and recharges may be made 4
  days prior to due date.

DUE AS STAMPED BELOW

RETURNED   SEP 2 5 1999

SEP 0 9 1999   JUN 2 4 2004

Santa Cruz Jitney

12,000 (11/95)

Lightning Source UK Ltd.
Milton Keynes UK
UKHW020817201121
394268UK00006B/1393

9 781376 174144